WORK AND I...

PRIMARY SCHOOL

WORK AND IDENTITY IN THE PRIMARY SCHOOL

A POST-FORDIST ANALYSIS

**Ian Menter, Yolande Muschamp,
Peter Nicholls and Jenny Ozga
with Andrew Pollard**

Open University Press
Buckingham · Philadelphia

Open University Press
Celtic Court
22 Ballmoor
Buckingham
MK18 1XW

and
1900 Frost Road, Suite 101
Bristol, PA 19007, USA

First Published 1997

A catalogue record of this book is available from the British Library

ISBN   0 335 19723 X (pb)   0 335 19724 8 (hb)

Library of Congress Cataloging-in-Publication Data
Work and identity in the primary school: a post-Fordist analysis /
    Ian Menter . . . [et al.].
        p.   cm.
    Includes bibliographical references and index.
    ISBN 0-335-19724-8 (hb). — ISBN 0-335-19723-X (pb)
    1. Education, Elementary—Great Britain—Administration.
    2. Education, Elementary—Economic aspects—Great Britain.
    3. Elementary school teachers—Great Britain.   4. Teacher–
    administrator relationships—Great Britain.   5. Postmodernism and
    education—Great Britain.   I. Menter. Ian. 1949–   .
    LB2822.5.W665   1996
    372.1'00941—dc20   96–19874
                                                              CIP

Typeset by Dorwyn Ltd, Rowlands Castle, Hants
Printed in Great Britain by Biddles Ltd, Guildford and King's Lynn

For Barry Troyna 1951–96

CONTENTS

ACKNOWLEDGEMENTS

We would like to thank the chief education officer and advisers who helped us in the initial phase of the study and other members of the education workforce of County Town, particularly the headteachers who made themselves available for extended interview and who provided us with essential documentation. We are especially grateful to the staff of the two schools in which we carried out in-depth case studies, Hill Edge Juniors and Christchurch Primary, who were generous with their time, even in difficult circumstances.

We are also grateful for the funding support for the project which came from the Polytechnics and Colleges Funding Council in its last days, when it belatedly recognized that there was no level playing field for research funding. Thanks also to the National Primary Centre for supplementary funds.

We gratefully acknowledge the support of many colleagues at the University of the West of England, where this study was based. Administrative and technical support was provided by a variety of people both at UWE and elsewhere, including Sarah Butler, Jacqui Harrison, Lyn Cooke, Clair Wardle, Richard Egan, Paul Gilbert and Tim Knowles. Thanks to all of them.

1 RESEARCHING THE PRIMARY MARKET PLACE

Introduction

This book is about primary teachers, their managers and the pressures of the primary workplace. It seeks to connect the large-scale changes in work that go under the umbrella 'post-Fordism' to the everyday social processes of primary schoolwork. In the context of economic changes that produce a tightening of the traditional bonds between education and the economy, we set out the ways in which we believe this process may be illustrated in the management–workforce relations in primary schools, and in the social construction of the identity of primary education workers. Studies that attempt to link global changes in the world economy to management–workforce relations tend to be located in large-scale corporations or manufacturing industries, not in primary schools. The picture of primary schools, including the images created by research, sets them at some distance from this world, in a timeless, self-contained place in which nothing much changes.

We wanted to see how that world looked if viewed from a different angle, through a lens that focused on the economizing of education. In this chapter we set out why we approached the research problem of understanding primary teachers and their work in the 1990s in the way that we did.

We felt uneasy with much of the available material that looked at primary schools post-1988; their assessment seemed to place too much emphasis on an unfinished process of transition, underplaying the stress and tension so characteristic of education work in the 1990s. We were perturbed by the positive tone of much reporting of primary school management, and the implicit endorsement of policy developments ostensibly designed to improve performance and re-professionalize primary teachers. We were also concerned about the extent to which improvement through effective planning and management featured as an unexamined assumption in the literature on primary schools, whose traditional cultures and practices were seen as ineffective, obsolete and labour-intensive.

Our experience contributed to our unease in the following ways:

- we felt that primary education in its pre-reform state had many positive qualities, and that these owed much to the expertise and varied pedagogic practice of primary teachers;
- we saw much of the content of post-1988 reform as harmful to that expertise and quality;
- we were aware of similar developments in public-sector services and their impact on managers and workers;
- we were sceptical of claims made for market-driven reforms and of the benefits to be derived from the application of business methods to primary school management.

The final factor that led us into critical scrutiny of the market's impact on primary school workers was our shared belief in reflective practitioner-ship as the basis of good professional practice. Each of us, in our own work as professional educators, attempted to foster reflexive and reflective practice to support thoughtful experimentation and review, and encourage the development of independence and informed judgement.

The context in which we worked, teaching competence-based, externally-driven training programmes, aimed at developing skilled deliverers of pre-ordained curriculum packages and deeply hostile to any social context or dimension in teaching, made the continued promotion of professional reflexivity very difficult at all stages of preparation for teaching, and also affected research activity adversely.

The erosion of principle, and the constant readjustment, trimming and restriction of good practice seemed to us to be part of a wider process of denial of that practice in education generally. We felt implicated in the process, angered and disillusioned by it, yet active in engaging with it in order to keep the 'enterprise' afloat. In reflecting on this ambivalence and difficulty, we felt that we could extrapolate from our own experience to that of other education workers, especially those in primary schools, who had made very considerable efforts to soften the damaging effects of rapid change on their pupils.

In so doing, we felt that we could construct an account of post-reform primary teaching that departed from the conventional wisdom that any problems in the system resulted from the process of transition, rather than from the very nature of the change involved. Indeed, we sought to identify the essentially alienated and compromised nature of professional work in the 1990s, in the context of very significant political, social and economic change.

Since the 1970s, education in England (and in many other parts of the developed world) has been in a state of constant change. This change has affected all sectors of education provision, and it has operated at many levels; it has resulted in changes not only in structures of provision, but in processes of teaching and learning. It has challenged traditional versions of educational identity for teachers and students. It has shifted educational cultures, and changed public perceptions of educational provision and their relationship to it.

Such all-embracing and relentless change, supported by strongly held (though sometimes contradictory) ideological beliefs about the purposes of education, has presented a challenge to everyone working within, or affected by, education. The relentlessness of change has affected all practitioners, in schools, colleges and universities, as they attempt to keep pace with versions of reform. Administrators at local and central government levels have little experience of the stability that characterized the English system for many years, where such change as occurred was incremental and where fundamental assumptions about the value and purpose of welfare state bureaucracies went unchallenged.

Much of the energy of those working in education has been channelled into coping with reform, in adjusting to new expectations, and to taking in the explicit and implicit messages about purpose and identity that the reforms carry with them. Opportunity for detached contemplation and evaluation of policy and practice has been limited. Practitioners concentrate on working out the best way forward for their pupils and themselves and have little time to devote to analysis of the direction and purpose of change. The nature of educational work, the need to focus on the immediate task of managing and motivating young people in the classroom militates against reflection on change in the work and its connection to overall policy direction. Such material as exists reflects concern about workload and the need for stability, as well as practitioner support for some of the policies (e.g. Campbell and Neill 1994a).

Researchers exploring the impact of change on education have had difficulty in keeping pace with the turn of events. Nevertheless, there has been a good deal of research and publication, in particular a burgeoning of management-related research and publication to support the successful implementation of policy-driven change.

Researchers are subject to the same agendas as other education workers: education departments in universities and colleges are insecure, losing funding for their major source of income, teacher training, and researchers have been demoralized by the apparent capacity of policymakers to proceed without reference to their work. Ideologically-laden agendas have penetrated higher education and brought with them a shift to contract research for government departments, again, with a problem solving rather than problem-defining character.

As we move into a new era of cross-party political consensus about education and other public-sector services, with major reorientation achieved, and more measured discussion about more limited sets of objectives, there are signs that the policy–research relationship is changing, and that researchers are moving into a mode of operation not dissimilar to that obtaining in North America, where academic policy analysts offer advice on policy problems.

None of these developments, however, encourage serious, independent academic engagement with the nature of change in education. We have lived through a remarkable period in the history of education provision, and there is a good deal of work to be done on making sense of it.

We have tried to discuss the way our motives, experience and thinking have shaped the production of this book. We must emphasize also that this is a group enterprise, and reflects a combination of perspectives and ideas, approaches and influences. Sometimes these blend together well, reinforcing each other, and at other times there is some tension in the narrative, reflecting differences. We have tried to keep the central thread of the narrative clear and consistent, and to indicate where there are differences and why. All group-based research work involves compromise and elides difference in the final product; we have tried to retain some of the feel of the group research process, both in order to give a more accurate account of the research and to contribute to greater accuracy in the reporting process.

Research opportunities and choices

The reform agenda presented the education research community with very considerable opportunities. Similar processes and patterns of reform have been visible in many developed economies, and in response to this, and driven by broadly similar neo-liberal ideological commitments, the comparative study of the impact of globalization has become possible, along with excellent conditions in which to note and assess the impact of historically-formed local patterns and their mediating effects on reform.

Work constituted within such a broad framework of enquiry contributes to a number of concerns in the study of education policy. It helps us address conflict in the field about the theorization of policy, particularly where debate has stalled or ossified in a turning-away from both economistic and cultural reproduction theories deriving from Marx, and in a *mélange* of neo-pluralist, post-structuralist and post-positivist ideas that emphasize messy indeterminacy. It is important to move the debate on theorizing education policy forward, and this book is an attempt to do so.

In what way can a small-scale study of primary schooling meet such ambitions? We argue from within a developed and clearly articulated analytical framework that derives from approaches to the theorization of the state and education in the social science literature. We do not start from the 'educational' problem, nor does the content of education reform provide the point of entry to our study, though it is important. As we have indicated, we see education policy as part of a wider policy agenda, which requires attention before we focus on educational reforms, as the pattern of education reform (for example, in relation to occupational restructuring) may owe a good deal to trends in occupational restructuring currently being widely experienced. At least it may be conceded that starting from this point allows us to test the specificity of education as a policy area.

The second layer in our argument relates to our attempts to learn from and adapt insights gained from post-structuralist and feminist theorizing and research on the construction and reconstruction of identities in the shifting and fluid boundaries of state and civil society. These ideas also resonate with 'cultural' Marxism, of course, but here we are not so much concerned with tracing their lineage as with opening up our chosen area of study to their influence. In particular we feel that the reconfiguration of 'the public' and 'the private' and its consequences for workplace relations and workforce management is of use and interest here, and we attempt to reproduce in the primary school the kinds of studies of large and small corporations, laboratories and businesses that have so illuminated recent changes in work and occupations (Gamble 1994; Law 1994; Casey 1995). We also wish to acknowledge our debt to Bob Connell, in particular for showing how fruitful it can be to set theoretical discussion alongside detailed personal accounts, as he did in *Teachers' Work* (1985) and in *Masculinities* (1995).

Finally, we have attempted to present our research as process rather than proof. That is, we have tried to set out a convincing account, in which we identify a problem (briefly, the impact of market-oriented management on the autonomy and identity of education workers in primary schools), place it in the (theorized) context of occupational change, and identify issues and topics that sustain further exploration and illumination of that 'problem'. At all stages in the process of the research we made choices that were guided by a mixture of theoretical orientation, past (personal) research history, and 'gut feeling' about interpretation and significance (Seddon 1996). We think it is possible to argue that most research is done in this way, but that the rough and ready nature of the process is largely concealed in conventional accounts that use distancing vocabularies and techniques to create an appearance of objectivity and completeness. In working on this project, we have also worked through a number of implicit and explicit assumptions about the nature of research and the reporting of research, with the following consequences:

- that we want to acknowledge that the research is theory-driven, and so leads to choices about the avenues of exploration that make sense in relation to our theoretical concerns;

- that we acknowledge a link between theory and value; put briefly, we are opposed to the divisive effects of marketization and to the negative and stressful impact of enhanced managerialism on education workers' lives and careers;
- that we make no claims to produce a 'complete' account of particular primary schools; our account is partial, we are engaged with it and part of it as education workers ourselves;
- we defend that partiality and engagement, making use of the arguments of feminist researchers in relation to conventional research (Roberts 1993; Stanley and Wise 1993). We believe that this approach allows us to acknowledge and give status to experience that is otherwise excluded or denied, here we feel that the stance is of particular significance given the gendered nature of the management/workforce relationship.

These, then, are the arguments that support our orientation to the project and that shaped the research process and this account of it.

Education and social science

We need at this point to develop further our arguments for seeing education as part of a broader arena for social policy and social, political and economic change.

We see education as part of a larger pattern of provision, responding to, and affected by, changed political, social and economic priorities. We believe it to be a particularly interesting site for exploration of policy development and policy consequences, because it carries so many expectations within it, and because it so clearly reflects dominant ideological assumptions about desirable social processes and outcomes, and about the allocation of opportunity – indeed about the definition of opportunity.

Education – patterns of education provision and varieties of educational experience – offers an unrivalled site for the exploration of some of the major issues in the social sciences, and social-science thinking helps to clarify the tensions, dilemmas and contradictions apparent in investigations of change in education. In this case, for example, we have drawn on ideas about post-Fordism to construct a framework for thinking about change in educational work. We have made use of ideas about the changing nature of the global economy to interrogate policy change in the patterns and process of education provision designed to establish clearer education–economy links. Indeed we can track changes in organizational cultures and in patterns of work back into the organization and patterning of education provision, and explore the consequences for pupils, students and teachers. In doing this, we suggest that we at least explore the connections between macro-social change and the primary school, and also test some of the assumptions made by theorists about the direction and strength of policy-related change.

This book, therefore, sets out to do a number of things. Most straightforwardly, it reports the detailed results of extended observation and interviews in primary schools in an English county town. These data tell us about the working lives of some headteachers, teachers and other school staff in primary schools in one area of England in the mid-1990s. They also tell us about the impact on schools of policy designed to enhance parental choice of provision. We shall look at schools' responses to pressures to compete, to market themselves and to respond to parental demand. This is an interesting and relatively under-researched area, since most of the work on markets in education and the impact of parental choice has concentrated on secondary schooling.

However, as we have indicated, the intentions of the book and of the project on which it is based are not limited to the description and discussion of market-related activity in primary schools in a specific locality, interesting though we believe that to be. We want to move beyond the surface indicators of the impact of markets on schools in one locality, and we attempt this through discussion of what could be termed 'the real work of markets'.

Markets, entitlement and provision

A significant part of our argument has to do with our view of the market as a basis for provision. We will discuss the nature of the education market in more detail below. For the moment we want to note the peculiar slant to the education market in the English context, which is revealed in its consequences for producers/professionals.

We are persuaded that the policy agenda for education and other key areas of public-sector service is driven by commitment to neo-liberal (marketized) principles not only in pursuit of choice as a vehicle for improvement, but as a means towards destabilizing professional bureaucratic expertise and diminishing professional autonomy. If the consumer is to prevail, then the producer's influence must diminish. This is part of the neo-liberal policy agenda.

The concern to disempower producers, in particular education producers, who are held responsible for economic and social ills, has led to the particular form of marketization that we see taking shape in English education. Although the neo-liberal agenda has ascendancy throughout the developed world in the 1990s, there are considerable 'local' variations in its implementation, and one of the most interesting lies in the policy agenda for the professional workers who deliver public-sector services. In the English context, we would argue that policy for professionals is strongly regulatory, marking an unprecedented degree of external supervision, regulation and judgement of performance. All of this is apparently intended to enhance performance, but it is also a mechanism of cultural and moral control. We will discuss briefly below the reasons for this aspect of reform, which differs from neo-liberal reform programmes in North America and Australia, and we will also briefly review the principal mechanisms of regulation in England. For the moment we wish to assert that in England marketization has gone hand in hand with regulation, and point out that we are not alone in this reading of policy (see, for example, Whitty 1989; Ball 1994).

Education and post-Fordism

This brings us to the next point in our argument, concerning the connections between marketization and major changes in the structure of the world economy. Here we link the ascendancy of neo-liberalism to the rejection of state-managed economies and the emergence of flexible regimes of accumulation. We accept the argument that there was a major crisis of capitalism in the 1970s, and that as a consequence there was and continues to be a transition from Fordist production regimes to flexible, post-Fordist regimes of accumulation. Furthermore, we follow the regulation school's perspective on the broader socio-political aspects of regimes of accumulation, and the social and institutional forms that constitute a 'mode of regulation', impacting on individual behaviour and institutional cultures. Such a transition had very considerable consequences for social formation, state organization and work processes (Aglietta 1976; Jessop 1990; Watkins 1994).

The period of policy change in education, and in other areas, may then be seen in the context of redefinition of relationships between the state, the economy and civil society, with a small strong state 'steering' the market in order to achieve the 'economizing' of education (Kenway 1994). The 'economizing' process has very considerable consequences for education systems, which may be summarized as follows:

- that flexible accumulation regimes make direct demands on the education system for the production of differentially-skilled workers;
- as a consequence changes take place in the education policy process, and new production rules of public policy formulation emerge (Soucek 1994) in which corporate interests play a strengthened role in policy formulation and implementation;
- as a consequence changes take place in the governance, management and institutional forms through which flexibility is delivered; in parti-

cular new structures and processes, especially those associated with the flexible firm (Atkinson 1984; Watkins 1994), are introduced.

In education, as in other public-sector services, these changes reflect the abandonment of the Fordist state, with its population of bureaucratic professionals and its hierarchical forms of organization, in favour of new forms of state–civil society relationship, in which the favoured status of the expert service class no longer obtains. New work forms and new forms of worker – adaptable, collegial and responsive – are required.

Marketization drives this change, and a key issue for our purposes is the considerably enhanced role of management in delivering this market-driven change, particularly within institutions. We see management, more properly managerialism, as charged with bringing about the cultural transformation that shifts professional identities in order to make them responsive to client demand and external judgement. Managerialism promotes the flexible and diverse post-Fordist provision of education by operationalizing it within the educational workplace. Managerialism acts discursively to internalize and justify very fundamental changes in professional practice, and to harness energy and discourage dissent. In our research, therefore, we have looked beyond the immediate indicators of market-related behaviour in primary schools to the internal dynamics of the schools. In particular we explore a number of dimensions of management and workforce behaviour that we interpret as indicative of management's enhanced role in steering market-driven systems.

Post-Fordist work and identity: the case of teachers

In Chapter 2 we discuss the consequences of post-Fordism for organizational forms and processes in education, as a preliminary stage in our investigation of management–workforce relations in the post-Fordist school. Primary schools may seem very distant from economically-driven conceptualizations of work organization as flexible, adaptable and responsive, but they have experienced considerable change in recent years, and that change has challenged conventional versions of public sector, public service professionalism.

As we shall see, researchers have paid little attention to the nature of primary teachers' work as work; 'common sense' assumptions abound in the literature. What is generally noted is some version of service as an informing and guiding principle, explaining professional orientation and contributing to patterns of work relationship that traditionally permitted considerable workplace (i.e. classroom) autonomy. Professional culture, bureaucratized and gendered, provided considerable solidarity and constructed identity. Primary school teachers were primarily effective socializers of children.

The recent disruption of that version of the primary professional identity has very significant consequences for primary teachers. The growth of management, allied to and responsible for the construction of new work regimes and cultures, produces not just rapid change but destabilization. The new model primary teacher has been released from the constraints of classroom-bound identity and her status as expert provider challenged by outside authority. Her responsibilities are without limit, as is her capacity to contribute to improved performance. Her identity, previously constructed through a mix of wide professional resources, for example training and local authority support, and combined with a local element constructed in relationship with her 'class', is now exclusively school-focused. She is at once more constrained (in terms of support and opportunities) and more extended (in terms of responsibilities).

The nature of primary teachers' responses to change and their ambivalence about it reflect wider changes and ambivalences in the public-sector services, as they become post-Fordist forms, and internalize post-Fordist regimes of control. Primary teachers' work and primary teachers' identity have changed, and in this book we attempt to portray that change, and reveal something of the difficulty and discomfort of transition for some teachers.

That does not mean that we have selected data to illustrate our theoretical inclinations. It does mean that we think it is valid to attempt to explore education, and in this case, the traditionally insulated world of primary provision, from a perspective informed both by ideas about changed expectations of education, and by ideas about education–economy links and post-Fordist organization (Shilling 1989; Brown and Lauder, 1992). But we present the data as we found them. They may be interpreted to suggest that every primary school is affected by this transition, and that is how we have made sense of some of our material. We offer this as one interpretation, acknowledging that others may see things differently. We are also careful to acknowledge the complexity of the relationship between macro-social events, large-scale theorising, and empirical data relating to a few schools in one small town in England in 1992–4. The data are illuminative and suggestive, and add a different dimension to discussions of change in the sector.

The book juxtaposes theoretical discussion and empirical data on markets, management and work. We begin by elaborating some of the ideas introduced here, and discuss marketization as a vehicle for changes in state formation and the dismantling of producer-led bureaucratic structures. We discuss the consequences of such changes for the interpretation of education policy, and for the understanding of the education market. We then focus on the market, and on the various policy mechanisms that have led to change in education provision and to changes in relationships between providers. We also explore the associated shifts in definition and meaning that marketization brings with it. Next we shift the focus to the fieldwork, and to the meaning of the market in a small county town.

We then look in detail at the consequences of these processes for professional identity and at the policy mechanisms that have restructured teaching as an occupation. This leads us to a consideration of the significance of management and of the connections between marketization and new managerial discourses. The first half ends with a discussion of our data on the case-study schools, their market position and market-led behaviour.

The second part of the book moves from treatment of the market in the local and institutional context to analysis and description of management and managerialism in the case-study schools. We look in detail at the work definitions and processes of the case-study headteachers. Detailed discussion of management/staff relations then follows, and we test the significance of new discourses of management as carriers of the economizing agenda, against the experience of teachers and other schools' staff. We conclude with a discussion of the theoretical basis of our focus on work and with an evaluation of our approach and of its contribution to the understanding of education policy.

Before moving to the next chapter, we set out the research design and research methodology.

The project design

We set out below the project design and explain the comparative element of the project, in that in addition to primary schools, some limited work was done on residential nursing homes and restaurants within the defined market place. We explain the basis on which we selected the project town as a single discrete market and we discuss the focus of our data collection and analysis. We also attempt to explain the ways in which our theoretical orientation shaped the form and process of investigation.

Comparative basis

The project was designed as a comparative study of small service providers with a focus on the special case of primary schools. Parallel studies of nursing homes and fast-food restaurants provided comparisons with similar small, partially-regulated service providers. We selected these providers because while we were preoccupied with the impact of marketization on education, we felt strongly that comparative studies of providers with differing histories of regulation, differences in ethos, and different patterns of staffing but with some similarities in size and organizational complexity would provide potentially illuminating material on

the particular characteristics of education markets and their consequences. In reporting on the research in this book, however, we have
drawn largely on the primary school data, though some relevant comparative material on workforce–management relations will be found in
Chapter 8.

Market location

We set out to find a single education market that was reasonably self-
contained. We took physical features into account here, as a more concentrated population with good internal transport systems and networks,
divided into readily demarcated areas with boundaries created by roads,
buildings or natural features, permitted us to be more confident that our
study of the impact of choice on primary school patterns of enrolment
was located in a discrete market.

There are other factors too, that we used to help inform our choice of
location, which included the historical relationship of the primary schools
to secondary provision, and the historical construction of patterns of
schooling across county/town boundaries.

We located a county town that appeared to offer a discrete market
location, or as near to that as could be obtained. We then designed our
data collection in order to achieve a shift in focus from a survey of patterns of primary enrolment for the whole local education authority (LEA)
to the very close examination of individual schools as we shifted the
direction of the enquiry from the workings of the market in terms of
primary enrolments to the management of marketization and the impact
on individual staff in specific schools.

These different levels of investigation represent a gradual sharpening of
the focus of investigation from the broad picture of market-related activity
obtained across the city, through the more detailed analysis of the 12
schools, where we began to investigate the management–market place relationship, and into the final year of data collection, where we attempted to
establish the extent and impact of managerialism and its consequences for
staff–management relations and staff identities (see Figure 1.1).

The policy context and the research design

It will be apparent that the research design, as well as focusing on the
schools and their responses to policy, required that we connect the policy
context to our research themes and data collection methods. Thus an early
task for the project team was a compilation and analysis of relevant policy
documents that had consequences for the LEA and the schools, and
their integration into the investigative frame. We needed to establish how
such policy requirements were perceived and experienced by heads; in

Stage 1: investigation of impact of marketization policies, collection of data on patterns of enrolment in all primary schools (33) in County Town from 1989–93

Research tools: analysis of LEA data/interviews with LEA officers.

Leading to the selection of 12 schools reflecting enrolment trends across the town for Stage 2 of the study.

Stage 2: collection of data on the 12 schools, focusing on enrolment patterns, heads' perception of market place, market-related activity, relationships between schools, management structures.

Research tools: LEA data, structured and semi-structured interviews, documentary analysis (school handbooks, school development plans, guidance for governors, literature for parents).

Leading to assessment of the nature of the market place and identification of areas of focus for investigation of management practice and staff relations in Stage 3.

Stage 3: school-based case studies: Hill Edge and Christchurch schools

Research tools: interviews, structured, semi-structured and unstructured; observation of – meetings (staff, governors', parents'), observation of management–staff relations, documentary analysis (staffing details, budgets, planning documents).

Leading to assessment of data against theoretically-derived indicators of enhanced managerialism.

Figure 1.1 Levels of investigation of markets and managerialism in County Town, 1993–6

particular we studied their connection to entrepreneurial behaviour and enhanced managerialism.

This was a task that remained constant throughout the project, as policy developments continued to impact on the schools in our study. In our particular LEA, the backdrop of resource constraint increased in significance in the fieldwork period, as the authority fell victim to severe capping, and pressure to pursue grant maintained status (GMS) in order to secure more generous funding increases.

The most significant aspects of central government policy that were present explicitly or implicitly in our fieldwork are set out in Table 1.1, along with related indicators of areas of school-based investigation.

Table 1.1   Policy context and fieldwork themes

Central policy	School-based investigation
teacher pay/conditions	finance/budget
appraisal	staffing/promotions/resourcing
GMS	enrolment
LMS	marketing
inspection	GMS
open enrolment	curriculum
league tables	planning
information to parents	record-keeping
national assessment	meetings
	assessment

Theory and methodology

> There is no final arbiter between particularity and universality, there is
> only a 'good', persuasive, and by and large reasonable case to be offered.
> With this humble admission I none the less claim the academic privilege to
> analyse and interpret the lives of other human beings, in this case, at work.
>
> (Casey 1995: 198)

Earlier in this chapter we attempted to explain our orientation to the
project. Here we wish to set out briefly the relationships between the
theoretical ideas informing the project and the research design. The fieldwork – in particular the school-based case studies – was ethnographic in
its method, perhaps closer to critical ethnography in its attempts to reflect
micro-social context and reflexivity than to traditional ethnography. But it
was not theory-free, as radical ethnography claims to be. Indeed it was
embedded in a set of theoretical frameworks and beliefs, most of which
concern the nature of work in general and education work in particular.
The theory–data relationship is an issue that recurs throughout the book,
as we examine empirical data in the light of our informing ideas; the
relationship has been introduced here only in summary form.

Markets and primary schooling

Our exploration of the primary marketplace was informed by earlier
research that demonstrated the relative stability of parental choice of
primary school. We did not anticipate that we would find substantial
evidence of a competitive market for primary pupils, or of untrammelled
parental choice in operation. This does not, in our view, detract from the
importance of studying the primary marketplace as an arena in which
substantial change may be occurring as a result of marketization, not

necessarily in enrolments, but in the management–workforce relations in the schools, and in professional identities.

As we argue at greater length in the next chapter, the work of the market is not confined to introducing choice and competition in education provision. We believe that a significant element of the marketization project lies in its consequences for the work cultures of educational organizations. Thus the fact that we found considerable constraints on the operation of a primary school market in County Town led us to consider the work that the market was doing in reshaping those cultures, particularly the traditional cultures of autonomy in primary schoolwork, and amateurism in its management.

Post-Fordist work forms in the primary school

In the development of our research design beyond the mapping of the market, we were influenced by ideas concerning the impact of post-Fordism on educational work, and we have indicated the main elements of these ideas earlier in this chapter. Our assumption was that primary schools were not exempted from the more general changes in process at the time of the study, particularly if we took the view that marketization in this area was better understood as a vehicle of cultural change than as a mechanism of enhanced parental choice.

In moving the research design into the study of changing professional work, we also carried certain theoretical orientations forward. Put briefly, these encompassed a critical view of post-Fordist work forms, premised on the assumption that the main goals of new accumulation regimes are the maximization of profit and efficiency. We attached that critical perspective to the overarching framework of labour process theory, which gave us a particular perspective on enhanced managerialism and the emergence of more complex divisions of labour in schoolwork. The labour process perspective enables a critical view of new management discourses to be foregrounded, one that reads the underlying principle as enhanced control rather than collegiality and empowerment.

Within that theoretical framework, then, we were able to draw on research designs that explored the impact of post-Fordist work forms and their associated management regimes in business and industry, and to apply them, appropriately modified, to education work. We say more about the areas of investigation that were prioritized by this approach in Chapters 6 and 7, where we explore themes in the control and nature of schoolwork.

Theory-driven research

Our research design is thus theory-driven. Our approach to the education market, and to changes in the control of work, led us to concentrate on particular aspects of the schools that we studied. In summary form, the particular characteristics of our approach for the purposes of this study may be set out as follows:

- *Markets* are viewed as significant in their undermining of professional expertise, their introduction of the commodity form into education and their enhancement of competition among educational workers.
- *Management and managerialism* are investigated as the forms through which markets become established within the workplace, in particular their place in the control of teachers' work is a focus of investigation.
- *Post-Fordist work forms* are investigated through a labour process perspective that underlines the permeation of control through new managerial discourse, and is concerned to document the stress and ambivalence characteristic of re-professionalized workers in the public sector.

In the next chapter we argue our case for working within critical theoretical frameworks that concern themselves with issues of value and social justice, and thus adopt a perspective on markets that seeks to understand their discursive functions, particularly in relation to denial of professional judgement and authority.

2 MARKETS AND POLICY

Theoretical discussion

Before looking in detail at specific policies for marketization and their impact on the case-study schools, we want to set out some of our arguments about the need to understand education policy in a theoretically-informed way, in order to clarify our rationale for engaging with social-science frameworks, and to attempt to persuade our audience of the importance of theorizing for everyone engaged in education work. We do this because we feel there is a disconnection between much of the current research on education and theoretically-informed discussion and development around the issue of education and educational institutions, and their role and purpose in society. The gap between theoretical development and empirical work is perhaps especially marked in research on primary schools and their staffs, in which researchers pay considerable attention to documenting changes in work practices (see, for example, Campbell and Neill 1994a; Webb and Vulliamy 1996), but give relatively little space to seeking to explain and understand these changes. Similarly, there are increasing numbers of studies documenting primary teachers' stress and giving expression to their ambiguity and ambivalence in the face of reform, or recognizing their creativity in adverse circumstances (Woods 1995). Discussions such as these tend to work within a discourse of professionalism, which compounds the problem, as the theoretical parameters within which professionalism is approached in educational research are only narrowly drawn (Hoyle and John 1995).

As a consequence of this narrowness of perspective, and of a concern always to be able to demonstrate through 'hard' empirical data that primary teachers are ambivalent or re-professionalizing or in transition, there is a lack of connection to larger concerns about the purpose and pattern of education within social policy, or about changes leading to the redefinition of professional work in general.

For these reasons, then, we want to talk about theory. We want to make sense of the puzzle of what is happening in primary schools, but we do not think we can do that without connecting the schools to other social, political and economic institutions. Theories are no more than statements about how things may be seen to connect, how things come to happen as they do, and thus, to a degree, we all 'theorize' about our situations (and their relationship to policy), whether we are in a university department or a school or college. Some theories encompass more than others, for example, they may seek to explain individual cases (a burnt-out colleague) or they may point to patterns of phenomena (high wastage rates among experienced teachers). Whatever their quality, their purpose is to help us sort out our world, make sense of it, provide a guide to action and predict what may happen next. We construct theories routinely, by thinking about information we routinely collect. There is thus no question of divorcing 'theorizing' from data collection. Rather, the intention is to stress the need to look at what we find out in a self-conscious, theorized way, interrogating our theoretical 'hunches' and their associated sensitizing concepts while looking at policy effects at the macro-, meso- and micro-levels, or all three.

It is that dynamic relationship which preserves us from entrapment in static 'grand theory' or from endless accumulation of evidence. Recognition of the one, particularly when we are assured of the death of the meta-narrative should not lead us into the other. As Bourdieu *et al.*, put it:

A theory is neither the highest common denominator of all the grand theories of the past nor, *a fortiori*, is it that part of sociological discourse which opposes empiricism simply by escaping experimental control. Neither is it the gallery of canonical theories in which theory is reduced to the history of theory, or a system of concepts that recognises no other criterion of scientificity than that of semantic coherence and refers to itself instead of measuring itself against the facts, nor, on the other hand, is it the compilation of minor true facts or fragmentally demonstrated relationships, which is merely the positivists' reinterpretation of the traditional idea of the sociological summa. Both the traditional representation of theory and the positivist representation, which assigns theory no other function than that of representing a set of experimental laws as fully, as simply, and as exactly as possible, dispossess theory of its primordial function, which is to secure the epistemological break and to lead to the principle capable of accounting for the contradictions, incoherences, and lacunae that this principle alone can bring to light in the system of established laws.

(Bourdieu *et al.* 1991: 29–30)

Here we need to apply this to our work: we are really talking about having a set of coherent explanatory principles that form a consistent treatment of the primary school inside its broader framework and also internally, as a social institution.

We want to demonstrate how we used these theories 'to think with', how they helped us to 'see' the schools, what we found as empirical data, and what the data tell us about the appropriateness, quality and strength of our theory.

Here we need to return to the issue of values and theory, and their interrelationship. We have already indicated that we are engaged *with* as well as *in* the research topic. By this we mean that we feel part of the process that we are exploring. We are all ourselves education workers who have lived through the restructuring, and enhanced managerial and external measurement that we study here. Our reflections on that experience have helped us to think about the process in primary schools, and have encouraged us to move beyond documenting 'transition' and towards identifying explanatory principles that take account of, and account for, our experience of alienation, demoralization and loss of autonomy.

We are concerned about the consequences for people of this experience; extrapolating from our own, we believe that there are issues about power, exploitation, fragmentation and loss of professional identity that should be explored and illuminated. Again, drawing on our own experience, we also feel concern about the consequences of such policy changes for managers, in particular as they hold more and more responsibility in isolation from any educational 'community' such as was offered by the LEA, and as they are positioned at increasing distance from their colleagues. So there are two connecting points here: the first concerns the adoption of an engaged subjectivity in the research, as Stanley and Wise put it:

> Our experiences suggest that 'hygienic research' is a reconstructed logic, a mythology which presents an oversimplistic account of research. It is also extremely misleading, in that it emphasises the 'objective' pressure of the researcher and suggests that she can be 'there' without having any greater involvement than simple presence. In contrast, we emphasise that all research involves, as its basis, an interaction, a relationship between researcher and researched . . .
>
> (Stanley and Wise 1993: 161)

The second point concerns our general orientation towards policy in education and its impact on teachers' work. Along with Dunleavy and O'Leary (1987: 337–8), we find that value positions form the broad background against which theoretical positions are developed or selected, and these in turn impact upon the selection of evidence. Cox's well-known elaboration of the differences between problem-solving theory and critical theory is important here:

Theory is always *for* someone and *for* some purpose. All theories have a perspective. Perspectives derive from a position in time and space. The world is seen from a standpoint definable in terms of national or social class, of dominance or subordination, of rising or declining power, of a sense of immobility or of present crisis, of past experience, and of hopes and expectations for the future. Of course, sophisticated theory is never just the expression of a perspective. The more sophisticated a theory is, the more it reflects upon and transcends it own perspective, but the initial perspective is always contained within a theory and is relevant to its explication. There is, accordingly, no such thing as theory in itself, divorced from a standpoint in time and space. When any theory so represents itself, it is the more important to examine it as ideology, and to lay bare its concealed perspective . . .

Theory can serve two distinct purposes. One is a simple, direct response, to be a guide to help solve the problems posed within the terms of the particular perspective which was the point of departure. The other is more reflective upon the process of theorising itself, to become clearly aware of the perspective which gives rise to theorising, and its relation to other perspectives (to achieve a perspective on perspectives), and to open up the possibility of choosing a different valid perspective from which the problematic becomes one of creating an alternative world. Each of these purposes gives rise to a different kind of theory . . .

The first purpose gives rise to problem-solving theory. It takes the world as it finds it, with the prevailing social and power relationships and the institutions into which they are organised, as the given framework for action. The general aim of problem-solving is to make these relationships and institutions work smoothly by dealing effectively with particular sources of trouble . . .

The second purpose leads to critical theory. It is critical in the sense that it stands apart from the prevailing order of the world and asks how that order came about. Critical theory, unlike problem-solving, does not take institutions and social and power relations for granted but calls them into question by concerning itself with their origins and how and whether they might be in the process of changing. It is directed towards an appraisal of the very framework for action, or problematic, which problem-solving theory accepts as its parameters. Critical theory is directed to the social and political complex as a whole rather than to the separate parts. As a matter of practice, critical theory, like problem solving theory, takes as its starting point some aspect or particular sphere of human activity. But whereas the problem-solving approach leads to further analytical sub-division and limitation of the issue to be dealt with, the critical approach leads towards the construction of a larger picture of the whole of which the initially contemplated part is just one component, and seeks to understand the processes of change in which both parts and whole are involved.

(Cox 1980: 128–30)

It is evident that critical theory in relation to education policy is not implicated in the solution of problems, or at least not in the solution of problems defined by administrators and policy-makers. Working within a critical frame requires the researcher to pursue ethical research principles and to assess research activity in relation to what might be broadly termed social justice concerns (Gewirtz 1994). Does the research imply consent to or support for the maintenance, justification and legitimization of regulatory institutions? How does it treat arbitrary, coercive power? Does it support the development of human capacity, respect for human dignity and worth, a more equitable distribution of economic and social goods and an expansion of economic opportunity to meet need? All this might indicate that critical theorists have rather inflated expectations of the outcomes of their research. We maintain that research can make a contribution to the goals embedded in these questions in three ways. First, it can draw attention to and challenge the assumptions informing policy and it can expose the effects of policy on the ground, in particular where policies increase inequality and impact unfairly on particular groups, in this case, primary teachers and their managers. Second, research can set out to explore how injustices and inequalities are produced, reproduced and sustained. Third, as Harvey (1990) and Troyna (1994) remind us, research can provide illumination of injustice and inequity that assists change and challenges 'common sense' assumptions about the official logic of outcomes and indicators.

This discussion of value-orientation and engagement with the research project brings us up against the issue of understanding education policy, because it requires us to place this work in some sort of relation to what education policy is doing, and thus begs questions about what it is and for whom it works.

We start from the position that it is possible and desirable to provide explanations of education policy at a level of abstraction sufficient to enable generalizations and comparisons to be made, yet not so remote from the detail of any given policy that it has nothing to say about experience. In this case, we seek to connect macro-level explanations of the economizing of education to changes in primary teachers' work. So we need to understand the economic agenda and its consequences if the logic of change in the schools is to be understood.

New formations: the economizing of education

The phenomenon of 'economizing' education is common to all developed countries (Kenway 1994). There is considerable interest among social scientists in the nature of the education/economy linkage, both in terms of current dominance of the economic agenda (Shilling 1989) and the resultant changes in organizational form and process (Brown and Lauder 1992). There is also interest in the 'new production rules' of public policy formulation (Soucek 1994), through which corporate interests play a strengthened role in policy formation and implementation. Although interpretations of regulation theory vary (Aglietta 1976; Jessop 1990), they all suggest that there was a global crisis of capital in the late 1970s, prompting radical change in the political economy and a transition from Fordist production regimes to flexible, post-Fordist regimes of accumulation. Such a transformation, it is argued, had very considerable consequences for social formation, state organization (Jessop 1990) and work processes (Watkins 1994).

In the sphere of education, it is argued, 'economizing' may be detected in the market steerage (including devolution of resources) employed by the small, strong state (Ball 1990; Dale 1994), in the redefinition of institutions of governance as part of the attack on 'producer capture' and in the redefinition of relationships between state, economy and civil society (Dale 1994). In particular, it is suggested that the growth of education quangos, with strong corporatist representation, charged with legitimating flexible and diverse post-Fordist provision, presents a challenge to public-sector cultures of professional expertise (Barker 1982; Deem *et al.* 1995: Graystone 1995).

Our research agenda, then, follows current thinking about the transition in progress to post-Fordist regimes of accumulation, and the consequences for education systems and processes (Hickox and Moore 1992), and for those who work in them.

In the transition from Fordist to post-Fordist regimes of flexible accumulation, educational organizations have a key role. They are charged with the production of a differentially-skilled workforce, divided, according to Soucek (1994) into three tiers: 'highly skilled professional and other core workers; specifically skilled peripheral full-time workers; generically-skilled peripheral part time or casual workers'.

Part of the production process involves the mirroring by educational organizations of these three categories of product within their own workforces.

Soucek argues that there are three crucial areas that are focal points in effecting this transition from Fordist to post-Fordist schooling:

organisational restructuring modelled on a corporate managerial approach;

redefining teacher professionalism;
articulating educational outcomes in terms of national economic
priorities.

(Soucek 1994: 46)

We are particularly concerned to explore the impact of the first two categories – organizational restructuring and redefinition of teacher professionalism – from within this perspective, and to assess the extent to which
our case studies of primary schools lend support to this interpretation. Of
course the last category, that of articulating educational outcomes in
terms of economic priorities, has a large part to play in reorienting the
system, even at the level of primary school, as concerns about the standards of performance and level of skills of primary age pupils become
major policy issues.

However, it seems reasonable to argue that such a shift in schooling
requires more than a 'simple' adjustment of curricula; 'steering' of the
system requires that teachers do not subvert it, and creates a need for
more effective modes of control. From this perspective, new management
forms and new versions of the professionalism of the primary teacher
become significant elements in the process of transition. The diagram
below (Figure 2.1), which draws heavily on the work of Victor Soucek in
the Australian context, sets out a model of the post-Fordist school.

Marketizing education

In this section we review the various elements of policy that have contributed to the economizing of education, including its relocation within the
marketplace, and that have replaced its post-war construction as a public
good, delivered through the bureaucratic structures of the Keynesian
welfare state.

The discussion below is hostile in tone to the use of markets in the
service sector, and disputes on a variety of grounds, following Ball (1994)
and others, the arguments adduced by policy-makers for markets as vehi-
cles for improvement of performance and appropriate allocation of resource. This is not to enmesh ourselves in the 'sticky sweet lies of
nostalgia' (Yeatman 1990: 9) for public monopoly provision. There is a
strong critical tradition, to which we have contributed, that explores the
elitist nature of professional partnership and its exclusionary consequences (Gewirtz and Ozga 1990; Ozga 1990). However this does not
detract from our analysis of marketization as a class strategy (Ball 1994;
Gewirtz et al. 1995), designed to reinforce those elitist post-war patterns
of class and schooling that were threatened briefly by comprehensive
schooling in England in the late 1960s and early 1970s.

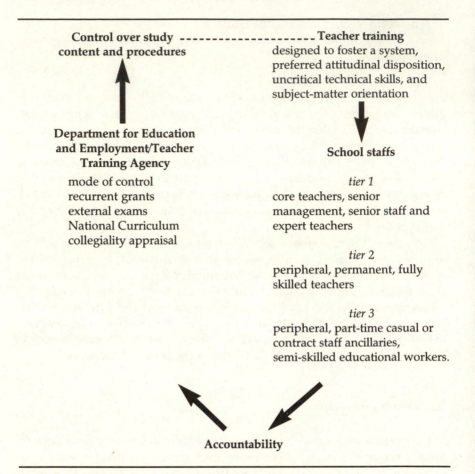

Figure 2.1 A post-Fordist school(teacher) model
(After Soucek 1994: 57)

We cannot review every item of policy that relates to marketization, but we will discuss the range of activities that are encompassed by it and use this as a basis for more detailed discussion of those aspects that have an impact on institutional management and on teachers. We are concerned to develop a number of arguments; in particular we wish to explain our view of the coherence of policy in relation to an education market. Here we see no contradiction between deregulation through such mechanisms as parental choice and devolved management, and the regulatory elements of policy, most particularly manifested in the national curriculum and associated assessment programmes and in inspection procedures. The regulatory form permits the state to maintain 'steerage' over the aims and processes of education from within the market mechanism. As Ball suggests:

the market form offers a powerful response to a whole set of technical, managerial and ideological problems, it appears to give greater power to all parents, while systematically advantaging some and disadvantaging others, and effectively reproducing the classic lines of the social and technical division of labour. It plays its part in the reformation of citizenship, as the mode of consumption is generalised . . . And it serves to generalise further the commodity form, a basic ideological building block of capitalist culture and subjectivity.

(Ball 1994: 10)

As well as taking issue with those who promote the market as the embodiment of fairness, we shall explore the peculiarly English intersection of marketization and the attack on producers. As successive Conservative governments have relentlessly pursued a complex, linked programme of deregulation and central control that has affected all areas of education, a distinctive element of English reform has been its preoccupation with regulation of producers – teachers, local government officers and central government officials.

The legislative programme of the 1980s represented an ideological commitment to the destruction of public-sector bureaucracy in education, health and other services. These services were established by the postwar Keynesian welfare state on the basis of entitlement, but are believed by the neo-liberal government of the United Kingdom to operate in the interests of the public servants who work in them. Much policy, then, is directed at the dismantling of these malign, inefficient state bureaucracies, and is designed to challenge the authority and the monopoly powers of the producers.

Here we would like to mention briefly the resolution of another apparent contradiction that is offered by this reading. This concerns the apparent resurgence of cultural conservatism, as evidenced in the academic traditionalism of the National Curriculum, aptly described by Ball (1994) as 'the curriculum of the dead', and the re-invention of 'Britishness' in the midst of a policy project apparently concerned with the 'economizing' of education.

Despite contradictions, there is an interconnectedness of social, economic and political markets that allows us to read this as a coherent project. Markets provide and reinforce economic and cultural advantage, and carry within them elitist (traditional) cultural norms. They thus play an important part in counteracting the destabilizing influence of education professionals, who are held responsible for social and moral, as well as economic, decline.

Having set out the basis for our approach to the market, we will now spend some time on its assumptions and their translation into policy.

Market principles

Common to all 'New Right' regimes is the underlying economic philoso-phy of neo-liberalism, that is, belief in the unfettered free market as econ-omically beneficent, allied to political ideas stressing the importance of individual freedom and the need to curtail state intervention/interference in individual lives. Thus the fundamental aims of New Right policies in education are to remove costs and responsibilities from the state and thus improve efficiency and responsiveness as a means of raising standards of performance. Putting education into the market place means making edu-cation appear more like a commodity so that parents are given access to a range of products from which they can select. In this framework, schools become more efficient in response to competition. There is a privileging of individual rational economic choice rather than collective political deci-sions effected through bureaucratic mechanisms. This exercise of choice is believed to be morally good, and reflects a rational and realistic view of the nature of society as summarized in these precepts:

- that individuals know better than the state what is good for them;
- that the market is a more efficient and more just institution for the distribution of goods and services than the welfare state;
- that inequality between individuals and groups is a natural feature of society and cannot be overcome by socially remedial action.

In this world-view the role of state agencies is nearly always malign. It follows that the role of the state should be minimized and confined to the maintenance of a stable social order for the full operation of the market, while a residual function in relation to ameliorating the worst excesses of the market also remains.

Accordingly, it is necessary to examine education policy against this background, and to scrutinize its contribution to the overarching project of stripping out state bureaucracy through the empowerment of the con-sumer. The implications of this agenda are very wide-reaching, and ex-tend to the reordering of relationships between state and civil society and the very redefinition of those categories. As the state shrinks, so the mechanisms through which policy is 'managed' and the relationships that embody those policies become paramount.

Thus it becomes of critical importance to seek to understand the pro-cesses of ordering (Law 1994) within the new policy discourse, and this directs our attention to the work of the market in education not just in reinforcing inequality, but significantly, in shifting the locus of respon-sibility for that inequality away from the state and on to the unsuccessful consumer and individual pupil. Let us look briefly at the operation of the social market before moving to consideration of changes in the state and education policy.

Here we borrow Dale's (1994) insight that the market is *conative* rather than *denotative*, that is, that it acts as a metaphor rather than an explicit guide to action, so that the market has to be marketed to those who will be caught up in it. Dale goes on to argue that there is thus a need to create a set of economic conditions in which markets can be installed at the institutional level, and a political need to provide legitimacy for markets. These political considerations set limits to the market form (for example, they explain the limited introduction of vouchers). The legitimacy of markets is pursued through a process of apparent depoliticization of education. What used to be collective decisions about priorities are reduced to individual decisions. As Ruth Jonathon explains:

> the recourse to market mechanisms to effect the kind of changes in the nature and distribution of education which would be unlikely to secure popular assent if they were introduced through planned policy is one aspect of the changed climate of education policy-making . . . the introduction of market forces should not be seen just as a negative procedure of rolling back the state in order simply to devolve power to the people, with government seeking only to maximise individual freedom. For by delegating to individuals decisions which, in aggregate, have substantial policy effects, legislators are not lessening the extent to which they direct policy, but covertly changing its direction . . . this procedural change in the policy mechanism brings about substantive changes in the nature and distribution of education, and in the general political economy, and takes such changes out of the proper forum for debate.
>
> (Jonathon 1990: 116–25)

The importance of the depoliticization is evident when we turn to arguments about the polarization of provision implicit in marketization. This polarization is the consequence of middle-class capacity to benefit disproportionately from social policies (Goodwin and Le Grand 1987), and, in education, it reflects the possession of more valuable social and cultural capital. But there are further factors that relate to markets in particular and specific ways. These are:

- the 'rational' choice of schools to select pupils and families with social and cultural capital, which contributes to the virtuous spiral of success;
- the privileging of parental 'exit' rather than 'voice' as a relationship between parents and schools, and the related argument, again advanced by Jonathon in her application of the 'prisoners' dilemma' to education policy, that parents will be obliged to make selfish, competitive decisions in order to gain advantage for their own children at the expense of others;

- the privatization of provision, so that individual parents may purchase some services, for example, swimming, music, school trips and even teachers, and thus reduce those available to those who cannot pay.

To return to Dale's argument, he maintains that these characteristics produce a multiplier effect that sustains and enhances polarization of provision, and renders schools vulnerable to the impact of the exercise of choice and exit by a relatively small group of parents. Schools thus become vulnerable to the loss of reputation, and are thus under pressure to conform to conservative, traditional modes associated with success. At its worst, this may lead to a mutually-reinforcing process of white flight and selective (racist) admission policies. There are further categories of pupil who may find themselves deselected by schools, in a situation of supposed parental choice – special needs pupils, for example (Gewirtz 1995).

These arguments suggest that there is scope for a critical theoretical reading of the policy intentions of marketization in education. It is well established that markets reproduce inequalities, and recent research (Gewirtz *et al.* 1995) illustrates this by looking at the differential capacity to 'choose' secondary schools. What this discussion leads us to seek to investigate is the discursive work of marketization and its implications for state–civil society relationships, as evidenced in the primary schools.

For marketization, in our view, is not a move from public to private, but a reordering of the institutional mechanisms through which state systems are governed. These remain state institutions, and their new forms and processes continue to do the 'ordering' work that education does for the state despite the apparent diminution of state control through the stripping out of state bureaucracies. We believe that what we are experiencing is by no means a diminished role for the state, but a different one, effected differently through different forms of relationship with the community and operated through the network of relationships embedded in, and required by, the market.

These are relationships of exchange and dependency, which privilege consumption and deny expertise. We look in detail at their emergence below.

Changing policy relationships

We have referred above to the creation of 'new production rules' of public policy formulation. These rules may be understood as new relationships, shifts in influence and power among established policy-makers, and new forms of engagement for those previously excluded. It is part of the market project to change the terms on which policy for education is made, received and understood.

Policy-making in England, 1944–95

It is relatively simple to set out the formal changes in relationships brought about by legislation and consequent shifts in control of funding or curriculum. What is less visible is the way in which the importation of the market realigns relationships in education. Table 2.1 sets out some of the changes in the control of education policy.

Table 2.1 Policy-making in England, 1944–95

	1944–74	*1974–88*	*1988–95*
Ministry (DES/DFE)	oversees	attempts steerage	Minister's instrument
Politicians	reserve	opportunist	dominant
LEAs	partners	squeezed	excluded
Teachers	partners	problems	deskilled
Parents	who?	natural experts	consumers
Industry	indifferent	concerned	partners
Pupils	invisible	problems	commodities?

(After Dale 1994)

The shifting relationships represented here are significant in their elevation of lay influence and their diminishing of professional expertise, whether located at the level of government department, local education authority or school/classroom. Thus we see the embodiment of the market in its privileging of the consumer and client, and in the case of industry the elevation of consumer to partner. The major policies that created these new relationships were very extensive in their scope, and included:

- school, college, higher education governance
- school, college, higher education finance
- school, college, higher education management
- LEA roles and responsibilities
- curriculum, exams, assessment
- teacher training (pre- and in-service)
- pedagogy
- teachers' conditions, pay, employment, career progression
- system management and structures
- system regulation, monitoring, accountability.

Marketization in education is most clearly visible in the provisions of the 1988 Education Reform Act, and in the Act of 1993 which enshrined

'Choice and Diversity' in law. The 1988 Act introduced formula funding, local management of schools (LMS), and the facility to opt out of local authority planning frameworks to become grant-maintained (i.e. directly funded by central government). The 1993 Act extended choice and diversity through the financial encouragement of specialist schools and through the acceleration of opt-out. Accompanying these changes in structures are changes in mode and method, as the National Curriculum requirements and the publication of examination results as league tables and of Ofsted school inspection reports contribute to marketization.

What is more difficult is to see beyond the formal changes to those relationships of exchange and dependency that characterize economized education. We will look specifically at teachers and their reconfiguration from experts to 'deskilled' technicians in Chapter 4. Here we want to highlight the removal of rule-based, neutral, procedural knowledge and practice from the policy 'grid', and its replacement by consumption, and political and individual interest. This is clearly illustrated in Gewirtz *et al.*'s (1995) study of parents as 'choosers' of secondary schools in London. Drawing on Bourdieu's conceptualization of education as a site of reproduction of social inequality, the study illustrates how possessors of valuable cultural capital can engage strategically with the market, playing it to their advantage, while semi-skilled or disconnected choosers fail to benefit, cannot act strategically, and accept the inequitable consequences as reflecting their lack of worth or capacity. Bourdieu's work is a powerful thinking tool for understanding how marketized education systems not only reproduce social inequality but make that reproduction appear natural, inevitable and attributable to individual failure to exploit opportunity.

But we can extend our theorized discussion of relationships beyond the individualized market-playing of consumers into the stripped-out arena of individual, atomized, competitive providers. These providers have been cut off from their professional bureaucratic cultures, and reconstructed as responsive providers of products. Many features of the policy agenda sketched earlier have an impact on this reconstruction of the professional and her/his relationship with clients, consumers and managers. Changes in initial training sustain common-sense, practical and local institutional interpretations of teachers' work and identity. As we shall argue in Chapter 4, changes in the occupational structure of teaching, following the 'economizing' agenda, contribute to the reduction of professional bureaucratic cultures of good practice, reduce autonomy and promote the significance of management. The current de-professionalized teaching labour force may thus mirror the stratification and segmentation of the marketized education system.

However, before we move further forward in our theorized discussion of the post-Fordist tendencies apparent in occupational restructuring in teaching, we want to move into the field, and introduce our readers to the primary market place in an English county town in the early 1990s. That is the subject of the next chapter. This depiction of a 'real' education market should facilitate an understanding of the further theoretical development which follows in Chapter 4.

3 THE EDUCATION MARKET IN AN ENGLISH COUNTY TOWN

Introduction

This chapter describes the research undertaken by the project team during 1993, in the first phase of the project. Our main aim in this stage of the research was to establish the nature of the market in primary schooling in our selected town. Many commentators have suggested that the operation of market forces in education, indeed in the public-sector services generally, is best understood, not through references to an idealized model of perfect competition, but as a quasi-market, in which increased regulation results in diminished professional/producer power and some forms of choice are made available to clients (Glennerster 1991; Le Grand 1991; Thomas 1994). We felt that it would be useful to pursue the nature of the primary market through investigation of the following key indicators:

- the extent to which planning and resource constraints determine the degree of freedom available for choice of school
- the perception parents have of their entitlement to choice and the basis, if any, on which they attempt to exercise it
- the schools' – more properly the heads' – view of the parents as clients
- the heads' view of the nature and status of education as a commodity
- any consequences that heads' views on these issues might have for admissions procedures, school marketing, and management practice generally.

These last points in particular guided us in moving the focus of enquiry from the operation of the market to the work of marketization on the internal relations and work processes of the schools.

The rhetoric of choice

It is evident from even a brief review of major legislation that parental choice is a key element in education policy. Parental choice of school is enshrined in the legislation of 1980 (Scotland), 1986 and 1988 (England and Wales).

However, we share with Bowe *et al*. (1992) a desire to explore the meaning of parental choice in terms other than those that merely 'test' government policy, and to seek 'to engage in careful investigation of the precise relationship between parents and schools as they develop within changing market circumstances' (Bowe *et al*. 1994: 65). With the exception of London, which has its own 'circuits of schooling' (Gewirtz *et al*. 1995), most research shows remarkable stability in parental 'choice' of local primary school (Adler and Raab 1988; Adler *et al*. 1989; Hartley 1994). We wanted to find out about the impact of policy on those stable patterns of preference.

The policy mechanisms for the delivery of choice are, significantly, the redefinition of primary standard numbers in the 1988 Education Act, which, through open enrolment, maximized the capacity of each school in order to maximize parental choice. This straightforward mechanism is reinforced by others that privilege accountability. In addition to open enrolment, LMS and regular reporting to parents, schools are increasingly accountable centrally through Ofsted inspections rather than locally through their LEA. The loss of local control is encouraged as more schools become grant-maintained.

A summary of enrolment patterns

The section below presents a brief summary of trends in enrolment in County Town schools at the beginning of our study, before we turn to more detailed study of the individual schools.

We started our enquiry in 1993 by examining the changing enrolment patterns and admission procedures for the previous five years for 33 city schools. Very few of these schools were experiencing falling rolls. The sample was selected as representative of provision in the town, where 18 per cent of the 33 schools were experiencing rising rolls, 76 per cent were maintaining their annual intake and only 6 per cent were experiencing falling rolls. We also selected for further study one school – Carlby – where rolls were falling and three schools where rolls were rising; these were to be critical case studies where investigation would require more depth. However, we were unable to pursue the investigation at Carlby. Instead we substituted a school which had suffered from falling rolls in the previous five years but where numbers were constant at this time.

Table 3.1 and Figure 3.1 set our case study schools in the context of the primary provision across the town.

In only 25 per cent of the sample did the intake vary from the allocated standard number for admission by more than 10 pupils. Our sample thus

Table 3.1 County Town: trends in primary school enrolment, 1988–93

	Whole city		Case study schools	
	N	%	N	%
Falling rolls	2	6	–	–
Constant	25	76	9	75
Rising	6	18	3	25
	33	100	12	100

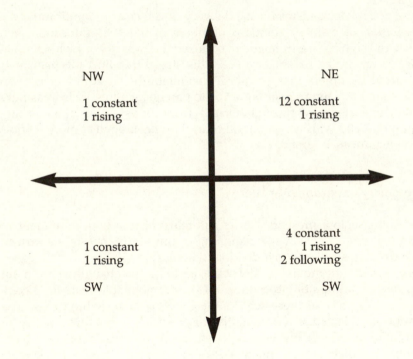

Figure 3.1 Geographical quadrants of County Town with numbers of constant, rising and falling rolls

reflected the position in the town generally, where 72 per cent of the schools were within plus or minus 10 of their standard number.

Figures 3.2 and 3.3 set out the achievement of allocated standard numbers in the town primary schools; Figure 3.3 identifies the position achieved by the case study schools.

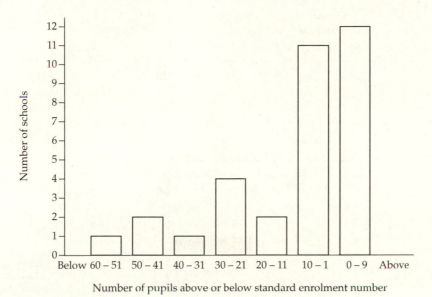

Number of pupils above or below standard enrolment number

Figure 3.2   Achievement of standard numbers in County Town

Open enrolment

Before the introduction of open enrolment the local authority in which County Town was located had operated catchment areas, as had most, if not all, local authorities. These were identified 'to prevent overcrowding and under-enrolment, to deploy resources in an efficient manner and pursue their own conception of social justice' (Adler 1993) The catchment areas had been designed to reflect the accommodation available in each school and to minimize the length and hazards (such as having to cross busy roads) in a journey to school. The majority of parents had always accepted the school within the catchment area where they lived, although the LEA was willing to allow children to attend schools in different catchment areas if this was possible. An appeals procedure was administered by the LEA and in the case of church schools the LEA assisted the church's own appeal panels.

This had now changed. The introduction of open enrolment and the local management of schools sought to create a market in which schools became responsible for the enrolment of pupils. This chapter presents the local market created by these changes through the experiences of 12 primary schools across the town, chosen to reflect the range of enrolment trends in state primary schools within the town, and through the experiences of the LEA officers whose role had been to manage the enrolment of pupils to schools. In the two years since open enrolment had been

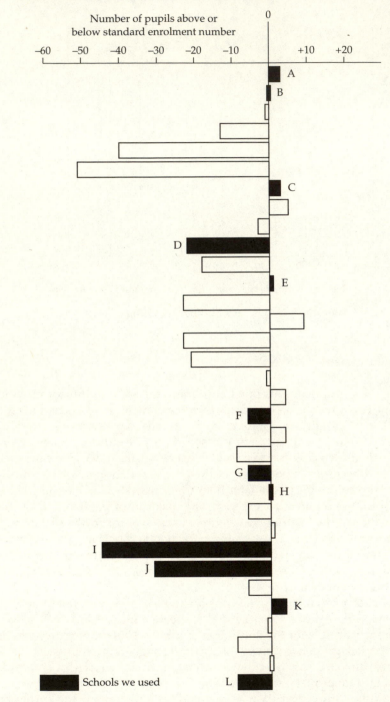

Figure 3.3 Achievement of allocated standard numbers in County Town schools

introduced, the relationship between the schools and the LEA was gradually changing, not only in the area of admissions but in other areas such as staff management and in-service training.

The interviews with the headteachers tried to identify the effects of these changes on their patterns of enrolment, the perception of the headteacher of the place of their school in the community or market place and the relationship between the schools which were now expected to compete for pupils.

We have grouped the schools to reflect the range of experiences we found. An analysis of the enrolment of pupils to the schools over the previous five years (i.e. 1989–93), a comparison of the admission levels with the standard enrolment number and the enrolment features of each locality allowed us to identify common trends. Nine of the 12 schools were now maintaining their level of enrolment and three were increasing their intake. We have divided the 12 schools into four categories in order to illustrate how for three schools this position was a cause for concern (group A). For the others, steady enrolment was a position which reflected stability and created confidence. This was the case even where three of the schools failed to recruit their standard enrolment number (group B). Where schools were maintaining enrolment and had achieved their standard number the schools were full (group C). The schools where enrolment had been increasing comprise group D.

Group A (Marshfield Infants; Hill Edge Infants; Hill Edge Juniors)

The introduction of open enrolment had been welcomed by all 12 headteachers in principle, but none thought that it could work in practice under the current arrangements. The reason given for this was lack of spaces at the popular schools. New schools were identified by the headteachers as causing difficulties as they were particularly attractive to parents. Three of our schools – Marshfield Infants, Hill Edge Infants and Hill Edge Juniors – were particularly affected by the opening of new schools. The Hill Edge schools suffered the greatest reduction. Ironically this was because their schools, despite enlargement, had been unable to provide the spaces needed for the families from the nearby new housing development. Their catchment area had been divided in half and a new school, Meadow, had taken half the pupils.

Marshfield Infants

Marshfield Infants was situated in a middle-class residential area. It had traditionally taken children from the local education authority catchment area and beyond. Parents from the Carlby area, a predominantly working-class area, on appeal had been allowed to take up surplus places. With development of new housing at the edge of the Carlby area this overspill had increased as the Carlby schools had been unable to cope. Now a new school, Deer Park Primary, had been opened. This had reduced the number of pupils coming to the Carlby and Marshfield schools and for the first time they were only recruiting up to their standard number.

> I hear that Deer Park has taken the pressure off that area [fringes of Carlby catchment area], because they were wanting to come here.
> (Headteacher, Marshfield Infants)

The head had always relied on the LEA to manage the admissions to her school and was now reluctant to take over this responsibility herself.

> I do hear with some colleagues that they sort it out themselves. Some local schools, because their numbers are below the standard number, they seem to work it out amongst themselves. The technicalities of why we do and why we don't do something I'm afraid I'm not sure on that but in this school all our admission names go to County Hall and they negotiate with the parents.
> (Headteacher, Marshfield Infants)

The headteacher was fearful of the introduction of open enrolment as she could not believe it was practicable. She presented some of the difficulties that all the headteachers appeared to face:

> they [the parents] say 'The government has told me that we can go to the school of our choice'. And I say 'Yes, but the small print also says, only if that school has room for you'. And the governors here have a policy that it must be siblings first, then immediate geographical area. It would be very hard for people who live on the doorstep and find that they can't come to this school if they had registered early. But you are into a difficult area there, because you are into waiting lists, and what weight they actually carry. If someone puts their child's name down at birth does it still hold good over somebody else later on?
> (Headteacher, Marshfield Infants)

Hill Edge Infant and Junior schools

The Hill Edge Infant and Junior schools were in the adjacent catchment area on the south side of town. Like Marshfield they were maintaining admission levels but not to the level of their standard number.

> When the school had all the Meadow children it was added to and developed to make it a very big school. There used to be 360 infants,

ten classes, so it was a very big school. We still have the accommodation. With Meadow opening and Deer Park as well we don't need
that much accommodation.

(Headteacher, Hill Edge Infants)

The headteacher of this infant school also regretted the loss of the LEA
management of admission to schools. The infant school shared a site with
a junior school of the same name (which was to become one of the in-
depth case study schools). The junior school had also experienced a loss
of pupils to the new Meadow school. The headteacher, like the head of
the infant school, also regretted the reduction in the role of the LEA in
managing admissions, although as will become clear in later chapters he
had also welcomed the freedom that he now enjoyed in the management
of the school.

These three schools, although maintaining their intake, had been
shaken by the move to open enrolment. They felt vulnerable and powerless to increase the enrolment for their schools in the light of the competition from new schools. The response of the Hill Edge Infants headteacher
was to anticipate retirement and perhaps the inevitable merger of the two
schools, which would be unable to sustain the surplus places. The headteacher of the junior school, although feeling that the position of his
school was unfair, felt more optimistic, seeing his opportunity to introduce a business culture to the school and to enjoy his freedom from the
LEA.

Group B (Warren Park Primary; Christchurch Primary; Crescent Primary)

The second group of schools were also maintaining their admission levels
but were not unhappy with the situation, despite failing to recruit up to
their standard numbers. In these schools the shortfall appeared to be a
result of the design of the buildings. All three were spacious 1960s and
1970s buildings and the space had contributed to the setting of the standard numbers. The headteachers had no concerns over current recruitment. The problem that they faced was the possibility of not being able to
cater for local children.

Warren Park Primary

Warren Park Primary School had been built in anticipation of the development of a housing estate which was cancelled when plans emerged
to develop the other side of town, where Deer Park and Meadow schools
were eventually built. While catchment areas had remained the intake to

Warren Park had reflected local need and each year approximately ten children had joined the school, although the numbers could vary from five to 15. The large buildings had remained only partly used. Now that LMS had placed the cost of heating and cleaning the building on to the school, the head was pleased with the increased intake which resulted from open enrolment. A standard number of 25 had allowed children to join the school from outside Warren Park and the intake had almost doubled to 19. The school was now more financially viable, in the head's opinion.

Christchurch Church of England Primary

Christchurch, later chosen as our second in-depth case study school, was close to the town centre but with a 1960s building which had replaced the old Christchurch school. It served a very mixed community with established residential Victorian housing, high rise flats, new estates and a site for travellers. The headteacher was confident about recruitment as he felt families recognized Christchurch as their local community school:

> Families, established families, living in the area who, they themselves may have attended this school, have had a good experience or a satisfactory experience in the past. . . . It is the closest school. It is as simple as that – proximity to the home.
>
> (Headteacher, Christchurch)

Crescent Primary

Crescent School was in the town centre and was very similar to Christchurch in size and recruitment. There were more children from families of Asian origin in the school, as part of the original Crescent catchment area included the Asian community. The school buildings, which had won an architectural award, were placed in large grounds. Like the headteacher at Christchurch, the headteacher at Crescent Primary welcomed open enrolment but did not think it could work. He was not concerned that the standard enrolment number had not been achieved. There were two parallel classes for each year and more pupils would disturb the composition of classes. Mixed age classes would not be welcomed.

Group C (Warburton Church of England Primary; Wrighton Juniors; St Joseph's Roman Catholic Infants)

The third group of schools were all maintaining their admission levels and, unlike Group B, were achieving their standard enrolment numbers.

The schools were therefore full. The three headteachers were very different in their attitude to recruitment. One headteacher saw his school as a community school, like the headteachers at Christchurch and Crescent, in contrast to the second headteacher, who saw open enrolment as an opportunity to select his pupils. The third school was a Roman Catholic school, and therefore although their recruitment levels were similar to the other schools, their catchment area was the whole town and beyond.

Warburton (Aided) Church of England Primary

Warburton Primary was one of the two new schools in our sample, built to replace an overcrowded small Victorian building which was demolished when the new school opened. The standard number was therefore set by the governors, and open enrolment had allowed the headteacher to informally select his pupils. He had deliberately changed the balance of pupils that had existed in the old catchment area:

> I don't line them [parents] up and give them points. But to all intents and purposes you can almost say you are doing a bit of social engineering. Basically what I have done over the last two years is try and redress the balance between the very, very large percentage of problem and special educational needs children that we had here and the other type of child who comes from the more supportive home background. The balance now is about right.
>
> (Headteacher, Warburton)

Warburton had the advantage of steady enrolment from the rising population of the rapidly developing estates and the popularity of the new buildings, which attracted parents from the edges of the neighbouring areas of Carlby and Marshfield.

Wrighton Junior

Wrighton Junior was a large junior school in the centre of an established post-war housing estate. Main roads to the centre of the town isolated the area somewhat and prevented parents from using the newer schools, which were in the adjacent areas but across a dual carriageway. The headteacher was confident that the enrolment to the schools would continue and wanted the school to remain a local community school.

St Joseph's Infants

The only school in our sample that did not appear to be affected by the patterns of the local residential area or the age of the buildings was one of the Roman Catholic schools, St Joseph's. This school had its own catchment area across the whole town and children were bussed in each day from the suburbs and from villages outside the town. Although the headteacher was confident that her enrolment was stable she had noticed a change in the attitudes of parents.

> I'm personally of the view that we shouldn't rest on our laurels . . . Parents are much more discerning than that now and although they are wanting high moral discipline standards for their children, they are also wanting other things that the other schools are offering like good standards, a pleasant environment, openness, extra-curricular activities, the way the school looks as you walk through the door, the general aesthetic appearance of the school. So I take all that quite seriously.
>
> (Headteacher, St Joseph's)

Group D (Deer Park Primary; Alma Road Primary; Penchurch Junior)

Only three schools in our sample had been increasing their intakes over the last five years. In the town as a whole only six of the 37 schools were in this position. Two of the schools had taken pupils over their standard number; the third had refused. Two of the headteachers in these schools were confident of maintaining their intake but the third, Penchurch Junior, was not.

Deer Park Primary

The second new school in our sample was Deer Park Primary, the school that was reducing the intake at Marshfield and Carlby. The school had been built to relieve the overcrowding in Carlby and to accommodate the children from the large new housing estate on the outskirts of the town. The head had not yet taken over the management of admissions but looked forward to this, and did not share the reluctance expressed by the Infant headteachers at Marshfield and Hill Edge. She was unhappy with the way in which the LEA gave priority to the local children on the estate:

> The school only draws in from a limited type of housing and then we don't become a proper mixed community, so I will welcome the time when that doesn't happen.
>
> (Headteacher, Deer Park Primary)

Alma Road Primary

Alma Road Primary was a large Victorian-built school near the centre of the town, isolated on an island formed by main roads. Like Wrighton

Junior, therefore, its catchment area had not changed with open enrolment. The school was now full to capacity, with temporary classrooms erected in the playground because the LEA had wished to support it as a community school. The school was in the position that the Hill Edge schools and Marshfield were in before the new schools, Deer Park and Meadow, had been built. Alma Road had been promised a new school but each year the start of construction was postponed because of the failure of the local authority to receive central funding. The school had a standard enrolment number of 64. The headteacher would have liked less: '56 would be an ideal number because 56 divides nicely into two infant classes' (Headteacher, Alma Road).

Penchurch Junior

The last of our 12 schools was an old school built in the centre of a large housing estate on the outskirts of the town, adjacent to the original catchment area for the Hill Edge schools. The local housing had fallen in value with the development of new estates and over the last ten years the school had seen an increase in its intake from families moving into the area. However, with the decline in house sales there was no longer the turnover which ensured the steady enrolment in earlier years, and the infant school which shared a site with Penchurch Juniors had seen a decline in enrolment, which would soon affect the junior school. The headteacher anticipated a school merger to remove surplus places in a few years and thought his early retirement would trigger this.

The primary market in County Town

All schools in our sample, with the exception of St Joseph's Roman Catholic School, had been affected by housing and demographic trends within the local area of their school. The effects of the old catchment areas were still strong with all schools, including Warburton where the head informally selected his pupils.

Only in two areas of the town were the standard admission numbers (set out in Circular 6/91, DES) not reflected in the class sizes of the local schools. In both of these areas, Carlby and Hill Edge, new schools, Deer Park and Meadow, had been built to accommodate the previously increasing pupil rolls resulting from extensive house building. In Carlby the standard admission numbers of the infant and junior schools were 90 and 95 respectively, but the pupils did not exceed 52 in any year. Carlby and Hill Edge were the only two schools in the town where enrolment had fallen over the last five years and the twin sites faced amalgamation to reduce surplus places. In Hill Edge the admission numbers were 107 and

90 for the two schools and the number of pupils in any one year did not exceed 62. Enrolment after the adjustment for the opening of the nearby three new schools had, however, remained constant.

The schools maintained the identities of local schools, often linked also by name to a particular district of the town. The heads welcomed this but some were beginning to move away from recruitment of all local children as they attempted to determine the balance or size of their intake. That these 11 schools were so greatly affected by the patterns of local housing suggests that they operated as community schools. As such they had the characteristics of the 'circuit of schooling' described by Gewirtz, Ball and Bowe in their analysis of London secondary schools: 'the circuit of local community comprehensive schools which recruit the majority of their students from their immediate locality [and] have highly localised reputations' (Gewirtz et al. 1995: 53).

The Roman Catholic School in our sample reflected the fourth category, 'a parallel, but separate circuit of Catholic schools'. The interviews allowed us to explore the extent to which headteachers felt their schools were 'local schools' and how this was being challenged by the introduction of a free educational market.

Although the headteachers recognized that parents now had a right to choose their school they did not see their schools as a commodity available to any parent. The largest group accepted the children who enrolled to their school without any attempt to restrict or encourage any particular type of pupil. They saw their schools first and foremost as providers of a service for their local community, but this was not entirely straightforward:

> to an extent the old idea of catchment areas did serve a useful purpose, but as I mentioned earlier, we would have lost children who would like to stay, purely on catchment area and that strikes me as being unfair. And I don't basically want children here whose parents don't want them to come here, so if there are children in the catchment area who would prefer to go to another school that's fine by me.

> (Headteacher, Crescent Primary)

The second response, from the headteachers of Deer Park and Hill Edge Juniors, showed that they saw their schools as providing a service for their local community, and yet they both regretted this and would have liked to receive a different mix of pupils. The heads were both in parts of the town where urban renewal and redevelopment were leading to disturbance in residential patterns as established communities were rehoused or dispersed to different parts of the town. This situation reduced the enrolment at Hill Edge as the children were moved to a new school, Meadow. The headteacher of Hill Edge Juniors was unhappy that it was mostly the middle-class parents who were now moving their children to the new school and at Deer Park the headteacher was unhappy that there was not a greater social mix of pupils in the school.

All heads in the first and second group felt able to describe the factors that they felt affected parents in their selection of a school. They felt that parents wanted to go to a school near to their home. They believed that parents learnt of the reputation of the schools from their neighbours and friends and this also influenced their decision. The existing rolls of parents registered at these schools supported the heads' view that parents were choosing the school nearest to their home, with the exception of the newly built schools. Each school had a few exceptional families who, for varying reasons, brought their children to the school from further away. One family, for example, used the school nearest to the children's grandmother, who looked after them at the end of the day; another family had moved house but had kept their children at the school close to their old home to ensure continuity in their education.

A third response, from the headteacher of Warburton, was to reject the concept of a community school and to informally select the pupils wishing to enrol at the school.

A fourth response was to view the school as offering a specialist service for a type of family. This was the case with the Roman Catholic school, where selection from a wider community was based on certain criteria related to this specialized service.

The headteachers expressed disappointment that the parents' expectations had been raised of a place for their child at their first choice of school and felt that their school should cater primarily for the children in their locality.

> I believe that in the primary phase of education the schools should first and foremost serve the families in that locality. And I find it very difficult in terms of open enrolment that there is a possibility taken to extreme, that a school could lose its identity within the community it serves and I would never ever . . . turn a child away if it came from Christchurch. That would present an enormous dilemma.
>
> (Headteacher, Christchurch)

Other changes had coincided with the introduction of open enrolment. These included a greater autonomy for the school as a result of devolved funding. Another headteacher felt that the Parent's Charter had led to increased consultation with parents. A new head in one of our sample schools had completely reorganized the school and many of the changes, presentation and display for example, were aimed at attracting parents.

There were a few features of each school which the headteachers felt might influence parents in addition to those above. It was difficult to assess how much influence they had, but the headteachers thought it was marginal. These features included:

- facilities for pre-school children
- religious ethos
- infant transfer
- class size
- single year groups.

The headteacher of Warburton, who set out to select the children who came to his school, felt these features were more important than choosing a local school:

> They know we are fairly formal and have a tight regime. Also it's a church school and you get Christian families who want to come and I think the biggest thing of all is the usual word of mouth. That's what gets us a healthy waiting list. People like what they see, they like the fact that their children are getting a good education but – it's a very happy school as well although it's tight on discipline . . .
>
> As an aside, our SATs results are going to be a problem to me for another one or two years, particularly this set of results, which won't come out now, and the next lot, because they are kids who started and we didn't have any say about them you see.
>
> (Headteacher, Warburton)

A concern among the heads, given the amount of development in the town, was an inability to accommodate incomers. If the school was full because of parents moving in from other parts of the town, it might not be possible to accommodate a new family moving into the area.

All heads easily described a cross-section of their intake and none anticipated changes in the near future, with the exception of Warburton. The intention was to 'weed out' children with behaviour problems. He was anticipating the publication of league tables and was using informal selection in a way which he hoped would create a high score for his school.

The two education officers who dealt with appeals from parents and advised them generally on finding a school for their children outlined their perceptions of parental choice, and argued that very few parents based their choice on educational factors. They had noted that the schools chosen by parents were not those thought of as the most successful by the advisers in their programme of inspection. Even the school that had been identified as ranked last in a leaked league table in the local press (Gladstone Road Primary, outside our sample) was still increasing its intake. They argued that parents overwhelmingly chose the school identified with the community in which they lived and were therefore choosing the school nearest to their homes. They commented that schools did develop a reputation within their community as the local school and were identified with that community. They believed that this could lead to schools on housing estates with a poor reputation not attracting parents.

In a few areas environmental factors appeared to affect choice. The town was a patchwork of different socio-economic areas. Where two very different areas were adjacent the school in the more prosperous area was usually preferred by those living in both areas. A psychiatric unit which shared its name with the Carlby area and local schools had deterred many parents from choosing that school. Restrictions to access, such as railway lines and heavy traffic, also affect parental choice and had been taken into account when the old catchment areas had been created, as in the cases of Alma Road and Wrighton.

However, the education officers were able to describe other factors which they believed were also having an effect on the choice of schools. The educational factors which they could cite from their contact with parents included selection and coaching for selection, the teaching method within the school and the existence of mixed age classes. Both case study schools confirmed that mixed classes had become an issue across the town.

Selection was thought by the local authority officers to be of most concern. Some primary schools offered coaching for the secondary sector selection exams. However, where there was a nearby popular comprehensive school these tests were thought of as irrelevant.

The officers commented that some parents were attracted to schools where they thought a traditional approach was being taken. However, by contrast, a school that operated Highscope, an open-plan approach with an integrated day, was also very popular.

As indicated above, mixed age classes were thought to be an issue in some schools. They were unpopular with parents. This was also confirmed by the teachers in the case study schools, who feared a move towards mixed age classes because they felt it would be very unpopular with parents.

The officers had also provided information to parents who were basing their choice of school on the school that their children were likely to go to after the primary school, where links were established. This also happened within the primary phase, where parents expressed a preference for a junior school and therefore selected the infant school linked to the junior school. The private sector attracted many parents, with some driving their children to the nearby town which offered a wider range of independent schools.

The officers felt that where newer estates attracted families looking for an improved standard of living, these families in particular expected to have a local school available to them and not to have to move outside their newly chosen area. Four new schools, including Deer Park, had been built within these areas and were more popular than the nearby schools which originally provided for the children.

Where new schools had been built this was thought to be a major influence in parental choice of school. Where an old school and a new school operated side by side the new school was usually preferred. The 1940s–60s buildings, for example Penchurch, seemed to be the least popular. However, if the school was perceived to be traditional it was often preferred despite very poor buildings as at Alma Road and Gladstone Road.

Within the town centre the schools which had a family centre offering social and educational facilities for parents and the community were very popular. 'Race' did not appear to be a factor. Crescent School, with the highest population of children of Asian origin, was very popular and had buildings of an award-winning design. It was thought to be the buildings which were responsible for the high application level.

The second school, Hill Edge Juniors, where there was a moderately high level of African-Caribbean children, was not popular. It was felt that this was because the buildings and surrounding housing were of a low standard, a new school had been built nearby and families were currently being moved out while renovation took place. These accounts confirmed the enrolment trends at Crescent and Hill Edge but did not present the same perspective as the headteachers of the two schools. The officers talked in terms of popular schools, such as Meadow and Deer Park, where they had to deal with appeals and referred to the schools in the original catchment area as failures. However, appeals arose only when a school was full and unable to take more children and therefore only concerned parts of the town with growing residential areas.

Responsiveness to parents

All the headteachers felt that they had good relationships with their parents and that their school was responding to parental wishes. However, their responsiveness had not led to many changes in the school. Most felt that the type of education they provided was the result of the school's own planning and philosophy and that parents were happy with what was being provided.

Half of the headteachers felt that parents often failed to recognize the professional role of the teacher. One headteacher commented that he felt that this was a national problem. Three of the headteachers, at Marshfield, Alma Road and Hill Edge Infants, had experienced a conflicting approach to discipline, for example, in cases where parents did not recognize the difficulties that their child's poor behaviour caused in school.

Relations with other schools

In trying to identify how the creation of a market might be affecting each school we examined each school's relations with their neighbouring schools.

The only headteachers who felt that they were in competition with other nearby schools were those at Hill Edge Juniors, Deer Park and Warburton, who were unhappy with the mix of children in their school, the head who was selecting pupils and a headteacher in a school which had lost a large number of pupils to a new school. The Warburton headteacher who selected pupils saw this as outright competition for pupils, but the other two did not. He felt that competition for pupils, amounted only to a little surreptitious poaching whereas the other two felt that it was only a feeling of competition resulting from anxiety about future league tables.

Four of the headteachers, at Marshfield, both Hill Edge schools and Wrighton, mentioned the inequality of resources where a new school existed close by an old school:

> they opened with every imaginable piece of equipment one could possibly want. Now if we were given the funding to get some of those wonderful pieces of equipment and be redecorated throughout then one would say open enrolment was fairer. Now of course the government would say 'Ah well you do get your funding under LMS', but it doesn't quite work out that way.
>
> (Headteacher, Hill Edge Juniors)

The other eight schools did not feel they were in competition with other schools, nor did they wish to be. Some of the schools with waiting lists felt that they had no reason to compete.

Where the schools we visited were infant or junior rather than primary they were linked to a partner school. In some cases this meant that they had the same name and were on the same site although they were managed separately. Others were linked by being an infant and a junior school in the same area of the town. The junior schools relied on the children moving from their linked infant school and all organized transfer events to ensure this happened.

The only other formal link that we identified was between the schools who had an administrative link relating to special needs provisions or day care units, such as Christchurch and Hill Edge Infants. These specialized centres were attached to schools at the discretion of the local authority in identified areas of need. Places in these semi-autonomous units were made available to pupils across the town and were coordinated by the LEA rather than the school.

Other informal links existed between schools where heads were personal friends.

Entrepreneurial activities

Nine out of the 12 heads said that they carried out activities to attract parents to the school. This seemed unaffected by their attitudes to open enrolment. Of the three that didn't, two felt that they had no need to and the third, the headteacher at Alma Road Primary, felt strongly that resources should not be wasted in this way.

There was great variety in the activities that the heads described. None of them actually advertised or carried out formal market-research activities, or events designed only to attract new parents. Where schools already had waiting lists, one head explained how attracting pupils could be counter-productive: 'It would be selling yourself, to turn people away' (Headteacher, Alma Road Primary).

The headteacher who felt it was wrong to advertise commented:

> A lot of money goes on glossy brochures. I don't think it actually improves the quality of education for children and I don't think it necessarily improves the kind of information that parents are getting about the schools.
>
> (Headteacher, Marshfield Infants)

Many of the activities appeared to be events for existing parents, which the heads recognized involved prospective parents:

> Open evenings, curriculum evenings, I give talks to parents of pre-school children, the presentation of concerts, child-based activities and all sorts of things with the Friends of Christchurch, adult activities and they may be social activities to which other parents can come.
>
> (Headteacher, Christchurch)

Constraints on marketization

The policies of open enrolment, LMS, reporting to parents, the reduction of influence of the LEA and the increasing accountability centrally to the DFE had all begun to be implemented in the 12 schools. Despite this it is difficult to argue that a market had been created or would emerge in the near future for primary schools.

From the interviews it is evident that only the reduction in the influence of the intermediate democratic institution, the LEA, was in place for the schools. Although there was also evidence of entrepreneurship, this ironically coexisted with a view that the school enrolment was beyond the control of the school. The headteachers were willing to act as if a market existed but the conditions did not exist to reward their efforts.

That headteachers were willing to act as if a market existed when the likely benefits were so small indicates the need to explore the meanings of the market beyond the formal/technical, into its impact on educational discourse, on professional self-concept and on management practice. That the professional self-concept remained strong, and was informed by ideas of local community, is evidenced in heads' treatment of parents. In responding to parents the headteachers interviewed in our study felt that they had the appropriate professional knowledge to decide what should happen in their school. Their role in relation to parents was one of mediation rather than responsiveness.

Their priorities in relation to procedures for enrolment, i.e. selection of pupils on grounds of siblings already in school, proximity to school, and special needs, gave precedence to their educational principles and placed responding to parents in second place. In so doing they were acting in a way that many of the heads believed parents expected and endorsed. They felt that the majority of parents welcomed professional support and advice from the schools.

It would also be difficult to describe the situation of the schools as a quasi-market (Levačić 1994), since a 'number of competing agencies' (p. 2) hardly existed. Some of the schools may have perceived themselves to be in competition with other schools, but if parents were not choosing between schools but selecting the one nearest to their home then real competition does not exist. In only one of the schools was there an indication that parents were not always selecting their local school, and this was where a new school had been built nearby. Even in this school, however, the enrolment had remained constant. In all the schools it was only a tiny minority of parents who had not chosen their local school. The only specialisms were the long-standing provision for Roman Catholic families and local-authority-organized education for children with special needs, which, ironically, was threatened by the demise of the LEA.

Keep (1992) argues that the ideal model of perfect competition does not exist even in business and industry, and suggests that:

> firms recognise that the total unregulated competition of the economists' theoretical market creates levels of complexity and instability which make management impossible. Companies, all acting collectively, will therefore try to limit uncertainty.
>
> (Keep 1992: 36)

Collective professional identity has been the traditional position of primary schools, with the support of their LEA. As the study progressed, so that support was being removed, and instability was feared by some of the headteachers. We shall see in later chapters how scarcity of resources drives towards greater competition and how this, in turn, impacts on the collective professional and local community identity of the primary schools.

For the moment, however, having established the context of the study through this discussion of the primary market place in County Town, we want to move back to the wider issues of occupational restructuring and its consequences for professional work cultures and identities.

4

MARKETS, MANAGEMENT AND CONTROL IN THE PRIMARY SCHOOL

Controlling work

Post-Fordist work organization challenges primary school cultures in particular ways, as we shall demonstrate, while managerialism has a particular impact on the professional work cultures of primary teachers. We suggest that the marketization of primary schooling is significant in changing the workings of professional control and autonomy in primary schools, and that the range of practices associated with managerialism, and driven by the market, directly challenges traditional primary work culture and identity.

Setting the changes in primary schooling (and education in general) in context, we can see their origins in the decade leading up to the 1988 Act, in the changes in the world of business and industry. These changes re-established managerial control through punitive anti-union legislation but also by inserting insecurity and fear into the management–workforce relationship.

As part of the restructuring of British industry in the early 1980s, there were several cases of companies appearing to adopt macho styles of management, which represented a reassertion of the idea of the 'managerial prerogative'. In most cases this reassertion of the right to manage the workforce in a unitary manner was predicated on the existence of a common set of company objectives in the possession of management, which saw itself as the appropriate controller of this prerogative. Opportunities to re-exert this style of management were clearly related to the considerable threat of unemployment. This not only provided a constant reminder to workers of what was in store for them should they be made redundant, but further depleted the membership of trade unions. With a weakened trade-union movement on the one hand and on the other a political climate which favoured a reassertion of entrepreneurial values, it is possible to see the period of the early 1980s as one which represented a number of changes in management generally, with consequent changes in content and process.

At the level of political debate, the New Right presented a new view of British management along with its traditional pejorative focus on the trade unions. Though the latter were clearly identified with considerable inefficiencies in the operation of the labour market, British managers were also seen as contributing to the poor performance of the British economy. Initiatives were devised which would enhance the professionalism of British managers and improve their training and educational credentials. New discourses of business were necessary to legitimate the new management and its new practices.

The model of the flexible firm, so closely associated with post-Fordism, is important here, as it contained internal labour markets and a variety of employment practices. Greater competitiveness was achieved by the more effective deployment of labour, itself achieved by functional flexibility, where greater levels of skill were established by removing demarcation boundaries and adding additional tasks to the job. Advantage could also be pursued through *vertical loading*, resulting from decentralization, and/or *delayering*, which results in increasing levels of responsibility and control over the range of tasks.

Implied in all forms of greater flexibility is the commitment to fragment the internal labour market and create distinctions between the core, secondary and other sections of the workforce. The increased commitment required of the core workforce, it is supposed, is won at the expense of those positions removed from the relative security of this core. The implication must be that the homogenous labour forces of earlier organizations did not simulate the pressures of the market place by introducing enclaves within this labour force. The threats of substitution are therefore visually represented in the form of different groups of workers intermingling within the same workplace, each with their own particular conditions of employment to remind them of their position within the company's system of trust and value. So organized, workers live with the shadow of their use-value firmly attached to remind all other workers of the disciplining effects of the operation of the labour market. In this sense, discipline which had traditionally been embodied in the form of management, supervision and bureaucracy is translated from an organizational contrivance to a seemingly external imperative derived from the very nature of the economic system which lies beyond the firm. As a result, questioning of impersonal arrangements appears irrational as it implies a questioning of the entire socio-political landscape.

It is important to note that these changes in work and work organization have a particular impact on professional work, where control over process and pace is connected to expertise and knowledge, and the social relations of the workplace provide considerable scope for autonomous judgement. Although it has been argued that there is an internal conflict between professional autonomy and organizational needs, the emergence of the bureaucratized professional in the welfare-state-provided public services could be seen as evidence of a workable balance of autonomy and control. The new work regimes change that balance.

Professional work and flexibility

Many of these changes may be observed in the work of public sector professionals, to the extent that some commentators consider that we are now seeing the emergence of 'The New Public Sector Management' (see, for example, Hood 1991; Flynn 1992). This has seven central features:

(a) practical, 'hands on' management (not left to professional discretion);
(b) the use of explicit standards in the measurement of performance;
(c) greater control through output measurement;
(d) smaller, more manageable units within the whole;
(e) increased competition;
(f) private sector styles of management;
(g) greater discipline in resource use.

(Hood 1991: 4–5)

Comparisons of public sector professional occupational groups such as teachers, doctors and the police (for example, by Bottery 1995) reveal evidence of these restructuring effects, and close similarities in their operation. Bottery's study identifies the following headings indicating where specific policies impact on professional autonomy in those three occupational groups:

- retrenchment (reduced budgets)
- cost improvement programmes (through tendering)
- renegotiated contracts
- quality assurance mechanisms
- appraisal/audit systems
- diagnosis related groups (classification of students/patients/functions to allow comparisons)
- performance indicators
- resource management
- content control.

These factors were judged by Bottery to be present in the work of all three occupations and to be contributing to the diminished autonomy of teachers, doctors and police personnel. Interviews with members of all occupational groups revealed parallel trends in response:

- increased responsibility
- increased paperwork, interfering with the 'real' work

- increased stress
- increased entrepreneurism and control at senior levels
- little benefit at lower levels
- increased job insecurity
- preoccupation with implementing legislation.

These points are made to exemplify the substantial redefinition of public sector professionalism that has been in process as a consequence of the economizing of services, including education.

This shift has considerable consequences. Part of it is intended to deliver the flexibility and responsiveness of post-Fordist forms of organization, which have little in common with bureaucratic, professional organizational forms. It is not simply a question of mirroring new work formations in public sector services, however; there is a simultaneous need to construct a new model of entrepreneurial professional who will identify with the efficient, responsive and accountable version of service that is currently promulgated.

These new forms of professionalism are not held up by us as a stark contrast with a golden age of unrestricted teacher autonomy. Indeed, it is part of our purpose to explore teachers' work as *work*, with all that implies in relation to the control of work and the changing forms of control in different political, social and economic contexts. Teacher professionalism is a complex topic, and cannot be understood without reference to those shifting contexts. Professionalism is best understood as a form of occupational control, one that effectively conceals stratification and differentiation.

It is pointless, as Hoyle and John (1995) well illustrate, to try to establish whether or not teachers are professionals in some abstract, absolute sense. Professionalism must be understood in policy context. Critical analyses of professionalism do not seek to identify key contributory qualities but instead explore the value of the service offered by members of an occupation to those in power. The growth of the modern state and the development of modern capitalism in the nineteenth century produced conditions favourable to the development of new categories of professional. State mediation (Johnson 1989) created categories of state professionals incorporated into a framework of agencies financially dependent on the state. As public service bureaucracy steadily increased with the growth of state responsibility for education, health welfare, employment and so on, professionalization, as an affirmation of necessary expertise, grew in strength.

Bureaucratization and the fostering of education as a route to social mobility opened up the possibility of professionalism to a wide variety of occupations. The main points that emerge from such a critical, historically-located analysis of professionalism may be summarized as follows:

- the characteristics of professionalism are not immutable and professionalism has been transformed in conjunction with the growth and development of capitalism and the related emergence of the modern state;
- therefore the pre-reform professional may be most accurately characterized as a bureaucratized state professional, and it is this model that is being refashioned in response to changes in the state–economy relationship;
- some residual elements of historical models of professionalism remain and inform the conduct of the modern professional, for example, altruism or community interest. These may be used by the state to manipulate the employee or by the employee as a defence against such manipulation, and contribute to the ambivalence of professional response to reform.

The significance of these points is not so much that they challenge some ideal, essential professional status, but that they link professionalism to changing state activity. What we are experiencing now is just the most recent manifestation of shifting relationships between the state and professionals. The current transformation of the bureaucratized Keynesian Welfare State (KWS) into the small, strong state in the service of the market inevitably brings with it a reduction of professional power and status.

We may understand the emergent forms of public sector professional, the re-professionalized service worker, as contributing to the process of re-establishing control over services that had expanded to meet demand on the basis of entitlement. These services have now been redesigned and are offered on the basis of targeted provision. Control over access to goods and services lies ostensibly with the consumer, who is encouraged to exercise choice. The hierarchy of need that exists in the marketized provision is concealed and embodied in the worthiness of the consumer. Judgement about priorities, appropriateness and efficacy, once the preserve of the expert, guided by rules and precedent, is ignored or excluded.

This revision of professionalism across the public sector has very significant consequences for the nature of the work, for the occupational structure, and for the recognition and definition of authority within the work. There are also significant consequences for social solidarity and cohesion. The education workforce has played a historic role in appearing to allocate life chances through the objective allocation of educational value. Teachers, and other public sector workers, have interpreted this legitimatory function as offering the possibility to redress inequality and have pursued that possibility. Such aims have provided motivation and sustenance in their working lives. Their removal requires a redefinition and refocusing of the labour of teaching.

Teachers as a workforce

Tensions in the management of the teaching workforce are not new. Teachers are not only a significant occupational group but also a problematic one, because of their contradictory and ambivalent role in wealth creation, legitimization, selection and socialization (Ozga and Lawn 1988; Connell 1985). The state is inevitably implicated in the management of the teaching workforce because of the importance of teachers' work in these critical areas, but that management is always problematic. The concepts of professionalization and proletarianization represent, in polarized form, the strategies available to the state in the management of its teaching workforce (Grace 1985; Lawn 1987; Ozga 1988). Johnson (1989) has pointed to the need to understand professionalism as a form of occupational control, and Larson (1977) has connected its use in that mode to the growth of state provision.

The essential elements of these various arguments are that the teaching workforce is managed either through the promulgation of a professional ideology, which regulates behaviour in particular ways (e.g. militant unionism is replaced by responsible co-option), and which creates a climate of consultation and curricular autonomy, or through direct regulation, which permits curriculum control but which fosters militancy and reveals inequity. Neither management strategy is stable; historically each has led to instability, either through teachers extending the terms of the professional licence beyond permissible limits (Dale 1981), or through inefficiency and loss of quality in a highly regulated system (Arnold 1862; Grace 1985).

The historical operation of the cycle of teacher control is illustrated in Figure 4.1.

In the pre-reform period of the 1960s and 1970s we saw very considerable extension of the licence granted under indirect rule, as teachers drew on political and public support for investment in education to expand the operation of professional autonomy in pedagogy and curriculum content. Attempts by central government to exert closer steerage over teachers failed, and the emphasis on grass-roots development and innovation was sustained until the mid-1970s. It is important to remember the long period, from the mid-1970s until 1988, and the passage of the Reform Bill, in which teachers were prepared for reform, and the terms of their licence were renegotiated.

Blaming the teachers

In England and Wales, the Education Reform Act of 1988, a cornerstone in the marketization of education, was the product of more than a decade

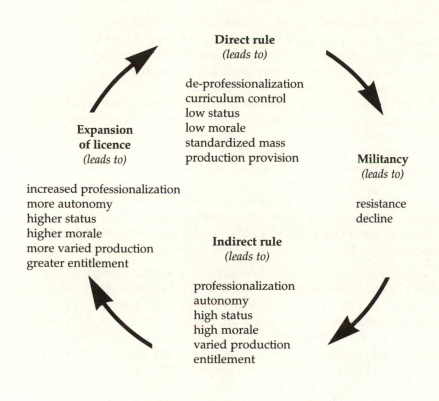

Direct rule
(leads to)

de-professionalization
curriculum control
low status
low morale
standardized mass
production provision

**Expansion
of licence**
(leads to)

increased professionalization
more autonomy
higher status
higher morale
more varied production
greater entitlement

Militancy
(leads to)

resistance
decline

Indirect rule
(leads to)

professionalization
autonomy
high status
high morale
varied production
entitlement

Figure 4.1   The cycle of teacher control

of intense debate and struggle over education. The decade of debate before ERA certainly prepared the ground ideologically for the major changes it signalled. That legislation, and in particular attacks on teachers' salaries and conditions of service and their negotiating rights, had also generated internal hostility, bitterness, disillusionment and de-moralization in the teaching force.

Thus in England ERA represented a key stage in a process which had begun at least a decade earlier. But in arriving at a picture of the long process of attrition which led to ERA, it is important to remember that the process of change began with the Great Debate of 1976, instituted by the Labour government of James Callaghan, which signalled the identification of education as a problem, and one that was primarily construed in terms of economic failure. Education's inadequate contribution to wealth creation was identified in the context of economic crisis and public expenditure cuts. Efficiency and economy were major policy aims, and the pursuit of economy eroded local government autonomy and wore down the professionals.

There then followed a significant shift from straightforward reduction of resource to the more complex agenda of 'revising the ideology' (Dale 1989b). Policy documents became preoccupied with standards, there was official endorsement of the view that they were falling. Progressive educational methods were more than ever held responsible for the decline. Progressivism was said to predominate in the English primary classroom, while secondary schooling standards had been eroded by cross-curricular initiatives which damaged academic subjects and by teachers and teacher educators in pursuit of illegitimate political aims.

The attack on teachers as political agents is consistent throughout the reform period. Teachers were said to be using the education service as a way of propagating left-wing views, views which were not supportive of existing social structures and which did not support capitalist values. The following quotation from Sir Arnold Weinstock, a prominent and influential industrialist, is a good example of the genre:

> Teachers fulfil an essential function in the community, but having themselves chosen not to go into industry, they often deliberately or more usually unconsciously instil into their pupils a similar bias. In so doing they are not serving the democratic will. And this is quite apart from the strong though unquantifiable impression an outsider receives that the teaching profession has more than its fair share of people who are actively politically committed to the overthrow of liberal institutions, democratic will or no democratic will . . .
>
> (Weinstock 1976: 5–6)

It is important to understand the centrality of the New Right attack on teachers to the reform programme in England. Teachers were, of course, scapegoats elsewhere, perhaps most conspicuously in the USA, where *A Nation at Risk* (Commission on Excellence in Education 1988) found teachers guilty of the equivalent of an act of war against the state.

In England, teachers were held responsible for most, if not all, educational ills, but they were held responsible for many other ills as well. Scapegoating of teachers was a continuous process, from the appearance of the first Black Papers (Cox and Dyson 1969). Teachers have been held responsible for economic failure, the breakdown of law and order, the destruction of family life, the erosion of traditional values. Such scapegoating is not a process confined to the tabloid (and 'quality') press, it is part of the language of policy-makers. Seifert (1987) has pointed to the Secretary of State's provocative handling of the negotiations leading up to and during the 1986–7 teachers' pay dispute. The settlement of that dispute saw the loss of teachers' negotiating rights and the establishment, through the Teachers' Pay and Conditions Act 1987, of a Teachers' Contract. As Seifert comments:

The Act gives unprecedented powers to a Secretary of State to impose pay and conditions on a group of public employees with passing reference only to their employers and unions. It coincides with general policy over the abolition of national pay bargaining, and the development of regional and merit payment systems aims at achieving labour market flexibility while dividing employees against each other. This process has already begun in mining, the civil service and the national health service. Its main purposes are to circumvent powerful national union organisations, prepare for private systems, and then force down wages through the competition of worker against worker in regional labour markets.

(Seifert 1987: 251)

Occupational restructuring

Occupational restructuring in teaching has taken place through two principal mechanisms, firstly the direct regulation of pay and promotion which has taken place through the School Teachers Review Body (STRB) (a quango appointed by the Secretary of State), and secondly through deregulation and devolution of financial control, which allows for greater variation in employment terms and conditions. The policy background, of reduced employment protection and an effective public sector pay freeze, is important for teachers, as for other public sector workers. Teachers' negotiating rights were abolished and a contract specifying hours of work and duties was imposed in the Teachers' Pay and Conditions Act of 1987, bringing to an end a protracted and bitter dispute which was as much about the control of the occupation as about pay and conditions (Seifert 1987; Ozga 1988). The abolition of the Burnham Committee and its associated three-cornered negotiations involving the DES, the LEAs and the teacher unions and associations set the agenda for a move away from national pay bargaining towards the setting of a minimum rate and the encouragement of much greater local flexibility. In 1990, a new pay structure was introduced, establishing a single scale for classroom teachers with five levels for incentive allowance, for distribution by school managers.

Automatic incremental progression was abolished. The 1990 pay award was generous to managers and deputies, and the incentive allowance scheme has worked in favour of senior teachers from its inception. In 1991 the STRB was established and policy since has confirmed the recognition of managerial responsibility by financial reward, and strengthened headteacher autonomy in allocating these awards. The third report of the STRB continued the pursuit of flexibility, of reward for good performance measured against indicators, and the encouragement of management discretion and control. The STRB remains concerned about the absence of career progression or recognition for experienced classroom teachers, and identifies this as a major factor in explaining withdrawal from teaching (STRB 1994).

If we move to the issue of deregulation/devolution and the consequences for occupational restructuring, a very significant factor in determining the developing character of the education workforce is the freedom of governing bodies to appoint as they wish, with regard only to the demands on the budget. This is a considerable freedom in LMS schools, while GMS schools need not adhere at all to national scales, but may devise their own. As a consequence new divisions are emerging, and the situation is further complicated by the use of ancillaries and auxiliaries (Lawn and Mac an Ghaill 1994).

Further incentives to flexibility may be discerned in the current and recent changes to initial teacher training, which permit greater variation in entry to the profession, including school-based training run by schools, and considerably shortened B.Ed. degrees for primary teachers (Landman and Ozga 1995). Teachers are further stratified according to their access to in-service training, particularly in the area of management. The virtual disappearance of financial support for in-service training (with the exception of limited national curriculum updating) means that teachers fund their own professional development; this effectively discourages lower-paid teachers. Taken together with women's double burden of work and family/housework, these factors combine to depress promotion opportunities and create a pool of under-trained unrecognized workers.

These initiatives, in devolution of financial management, in pay, in training, combine to promote flexibility, which may be exploited by the employer. The consequences for the occupation of the employer's use of this flexibility are likely to be complex, and we were pursuing our investigation just as these processes were becoming established. It is reasonable to anticipate growing workforce segmentation. Is also apparent that segmentation and specialization will not, in all cases, link automatically to deskilling, quite the reverse in some areas of secondary teaching. In primary teaching we may see the emergence of status divisions and the downgrading of the generalist. The existence of different categories of teaching staff provides flexibility to the manager and is potentially a source of increased power to governors and managers. At the very least the solidarity of the primary teaching community is weakened, a community which could be characterized, before these reforms, as exhibiting all the characteristics of unalienated, integrated labour (Bowles and Gintis 1976).

Management and managerialism

Before the 1988 Education Reform Act (ERA), influential research on the management of primary schools indicated that most school organizations were relatively simple forms with staff acting more or less as a team, under the leadership of the headteacher. Nias *et al.* (1989) described this as 'a culture of collaboration'. Although teachers were differentiated by salary scale (and later, allowances), this rarely led to visible hierarchical structures within a school's teaching staff, with the exception of the position of the head and sometimes of the deputy head. Teachers had considerable autonomy within their own classrooms, in terms of curriculum, assessment and pedagogy. This was consistent with the ethos and educational ideologies which predominated in the primary sector (Nias 1989; Proctor 1990).

This dominant perspective on primary schools as workplaces tended to focus on the 'integrated unalienated labour' remarked upon by Bowles and Gintis (though not, of course, in these terms). It is possible that absence of a labour process perspective on primary schools led to a somewhat rosy picture of their organizational forms and processes, the maternal culture of child-centredness could conceal the reproduction of patriarchal relations (Walkerdine 1983; Grumet 1994), or the operation of control reminiscent of a Victorian paterfamilias. The majority of the research literature on primary schoolwork tended to emphasize collaboration and close social relations, perhaps underplaying the operation of power relations (especially gendered power relations) in the workplace.

In addition, the lack of attention to the micro-politics of primary schools (with some exceptions, e.g. Pollard 1985; Newman and Pollard 1994) lent support to their depiction as simple organizational forms. Furthermore, their 'pre-Fordist' state as separate, closed, class-based compartments of production with strong worker autonomy resulted in a favourable reaction from much of the research/practitioner community to the importation of some elements of management. It seemed natural and sensible to build collegiality on the 'flat' structures of the primary school, and to break down professional isolation through teamwork.

Thus the pre-1988 literature on primary schools and their management created a climate in which change could be misrecognized as improvement, and failed to develop a critical perspective on work relations and micro-politics in primary schools.

The strength of the profession's commitment to the service of their pupils is well-evidenced by post-reform research studies. These illustrate the implementation of new procedures and work processes, the acceptance of accountability measures, and the acceptance of management responsibilities by headteachers. What particularly interests us is what this evidence lends by way of support to our view of the process as part of a transition to post-Fordist work, and what it says about de- and reprofessionalization.

As we have seen, several studies have constructed positive interpretations of change in primary schools; there is an assumption that teamwork fits naturally into the collaborative and collegial structures of the primary school, and that primary teachers will adjust to change once the pace has slowed, and old practices are no longer maintained in parallel with the new. More cautious commentators put the emphasis on transition as an explanation of teachers' confusion or overload. Thus a common conclusion is that there are elements of re-professionalization, such as collective, whole school planning (e.g. MacGilchrist *et al.* 1995) and the introduction of systematic assessment (e.g. McCallum *et al.* 1993), which are 'read' in a positive light, while other aspects, such as loss of control of curriculum content, are seen as de-skilling. What is absent from such discussions are connections to the wider world of occupational restructuring, and attention to the discursive elements of the new managerialism, which create a view of re-professionalization that underplays the losses involved in conscientious collegiality by invoking 'empowerment'. The research literature tends to emphasize the positive possibilities of re-professionalization and collegiality as outcomes of change in the primary school.

Hargreaves, in a series of publications (1994), argues that the new professionalism is an essential vehicle for school improvement, and that genuine collaboration is a major force for educational good. His conceptualization of leadership is very much concerned with the manager in progressive post-Fordist mode, ensuring commitment to common aims, and attacking the Fordist work processes of 'Balkanized' teachers.

Hargreaves is preoccupied with the necessity of change; our preoccupation with management is in its role as the vehicle through which marketization is achieved within educational institutions. Here managerialism is conceived of as the antidote to bureaucratic professionalism. The efficient operation of the market is fostered through the combination of legislative controls (juridification) and internal, institutional mechanisms, notably performance indicators and inspections, which ostensibly provide consumers with a basis for selection but more importantly provide powerful managerial imperatives. Marketization thus greatly enhances the significance of management. As Raab puts it:

> Government's hope must be that the implantation of the systems and ethos of management will take root sufficiently to legitimise new mechanisms and routines and to make them appear to be self-imposed, or collaboratively adopted, from top to toe. In this, head-teachers are pivotal, and a massive reaffirmation of their roles as managers is being undertaken.
>
> (Raab 1991: 16)

This emphasis on management again raises its importance in delivering changes in contemporary work, not just in education, but elsewhere. The principles of the flexible firm illustrate the opportunities for management of enhanced control of workers and their associated costs.

In teaching, the extent to which teachers are seen as a source of cost within the 'enterprise', rather than a method of adding value to the 'product', puts increasing pressure on those who run schools to consider cheaper substitutes and thereby enter into the same practice of creating internal labour markets even within an organization structure as apparently simple as a primary school.

In addition to the idea of the flexible firm, significant managerial discourses are Total Quality Management (TQM) and Human Resource Management (HRM). Along with other discourses, these played a key role in the early 1980s in representing a redefinition of management. TQM raises the level of measurable quality in outputs by introducing the previously external relationship between customer and producer into the workplace through the employment relationship. Employees are no longer simply workers but internal suppliers and customers. TQM initiatives drew the principles of the market directly on to the shop-floor with the discipline of the 'customer's gaze' installing an ever-watchful eye on the workforce. Under TQM workers were encouraged to adopt managerial concerns and behaviours to ensure their colleagues remained attentive to their tasks and aware of each other's level of contribution to the productive effort. TQM established a new pattern of relationships among workers. It required of them a level of concern which indicates a level of devolution of responsibility from management but does not appear to parallel this with any devolution of power. In the case of HRM, a range of techniques and arrangements have emphasized the employee's individual identity, bargaining and negotiating with their managers and being evaluated on the basis of their individual performance through the application of individual appraisals. This emphasis on competitive individualism echoes precisely the language of the market place, where the activities of the individual are his/her own responsibility, and where decisions are made on the basis of self-directed maximization. Under HRM there is no longer a need for third-party interventions in the form of trade unions. Management has generated the knowledge about performance and this will determine the rewards received.

It has been said that HRM is the necessary and appropriate managerial discourse of late capitalism because it uses the manufacturing of consent as a key principle. In Legge's words: 'Our new enterprise culture demands a different language, one that asserts management's right to manipulate, and ability to generate and develop resources' (Legge 1993: 40). It is this aspect of HRM that interests us, continuing as it does the theme of managerialism and management control of teachers. There are strong parallels with the traditional rhetoric/discourse of professionalism as a form of control, and similar tensions. HRM harnesses the occupational/organizational culture to the delivery of efficiency and quality. Mutuality ensures commitment which produces increased economic effectiveness and development. The tensions between individualism and teamwork always prevalent in professional work are apparently resolved by the strong corporate culture, which creates a cohesive workforce but avoids workforce solidarity.

The contradictions are in fact 'resolved' by the greatly enhanced role of management, and by its all-pervading nature:

> Strong culture/cohesion is achieved through a shared set of managerially sanctioned values (e.g. quality, service, innovation). Co-optation through the management of the culture reinforces the intention that responsibility will be exercised responsibly.
>
> (Legge 1993: 37)

The critical element in understanding management's enhanced role in HRM-driven systems is the extent to which integrated and co-ordinated activity is goal- or target-driven. Commitment to these goals is ensured by an 'enabling' or 'empowering' management. We have set out in Table 4.1 the main elements of HRM, contrasting them with more traditional organizational forms.

Table 4.1 A comparison of organizational and managerial cultures: traditional and human resources management (HRM)

Traditional	Human resources management (HRM)
procedural	driven by targets
custom and practice	values/mission
piecemeal	integrated
slow	fleet-footed entrepreneurial
ranked	performance
hierarchical	flat/flexible
division of labour	teamwork
sporadic conflict	unified

Ball's discussion of 'steering at a distance' and the precepts of the new management in his paper 'Changing management and the management of change' (Ball 1993a) is very close to our concerns in exploring the market/management connection, and like us, Ball gives considerable weight to the uses of management. The principles of 'steering at a distance' (Kickert 1991) discussed by Ball, where coercion is replaced by incentives, quality assurance and control, and repressive tolerance, have much in common with the discourse of HRM. As Ball argues:

> Management is disciplinary practice. But *importantly*, as a discourse management is productive rather than simply coercive. It increases the power of individuals, managers and managed in some respects,

while at the same time making them more docile. It offers flexibility and autonomy to some, although within the constraints and rigours of a market system and in relation to fixed indicators of performance. Management is both a body of precepts, assumptions and theory, to be learned by managers, and a set of practices to be implemented, encompassing both managers and managed.

(Ball 1993a: 112 [emphasis in original])

| **Flexible firm** | internal labour markets, functional flexibility, delayering, decentralization, fragmentation |

'discipline is contained in the very nature of the economic system reflected in the firm'

| **Total quality management (TQM)** | customer/producer relations introduced within the workplace, employees are internal suppliers and customers, market relations directly installed in work, devolution of management *responsibility* not power |

| **Human resources management (HRM)** | individual, not collective employee identity, individual appraisal and reward, integrated planning, coordinated activity |

'mutuality ensures commitment and thus economic efficiency; workforce cohesion but not solidarity'

Figure 4.2   New management discourses: the essential elements

The echoes of professionalism as a form of control are apparent. What is different is the shift in the locus of control, from a directive state, manipulating professional rhetoric in a relatively undifferentiated workforce, to the head, as manager, working within a framework of regulations, and using management of the culture to internalize controls and ensure compliance. It is in this context that we need to explore the meanings of empowerment and collegiality, as these terms, along with the proliferation of management terms, may conceal the increase in monitoring and surveillance of teachers' work. Market success requires smooth production and the eradication of 'problems'. Deviations from policy are less likely to be tolerated by the senior management team. Class teachers must answer to postholders, indeed the growth of supervisory functions implicit in collegiality, which may 'extend' professionalism for some, but de-skill others, particularly women and part-timers, connects to the bigger agenda of emergent post-Fordist production processes. The importance of these new management discourses and processes in internalizing control mechanisms should not be overlooked.

This is an extremely critical perspective on the new managerialism, and one that is opposed to the literature on restructuring and self-management that implicitly accepts much of the HRM and TQM discourse. However, we felt it was important to draw attention to the significance of management work, and its preoccupation with control. We feel this particularly strongly in the context of a burgeoning literature on school restructuring which accepts much of the HRM discourse, and misrecognizes it as an escape from the bureaucratic regulation and paternalistic hierarchy of modernity (Hargreaves 1994). It may well be these things, but that is not all that it is. In arguing this case we recognize that we are setting ourselves outside the dominant paradigm of analysis in educational management, that of the self-managing school (Hargreaves and Hopkins 1991; Caldwell and Spinks 1992). That paradigm is itself a reworking of the HRM business discourse, largely without the attendant debate on industrial relations and power that characterized its emergence in mainstream management. That debate continues, and is supported by detailed case study work that attempts to disclose what is really going on in the new industrial relations of post-Fordist, post-modern business and industry (Geary 1992; Scott 1994). Our project attempts to contribute to that debate, by including within it education workers and their managers.

5

Two schools: in-depth
case studies

Introduction

In this chapter we turn to the two in-depth case study schools which were
selected for closer investigation. Our reasons for choosing these particular
schools are explained. We then offer a detailed portrait of each school, its
history and its local context, including its perceived market position. We
explore the significance of marketization for each school in terms of its
influence on school culture and processes.

What emerges from the comparison of these two apparently contrasting schools is that there are considerable similarities between them in
terms of the experiences of the staff working in them.

Selection of the in-depth case study schools

By the half-way stage of our project we had examined some 12 primary
schools in County Town through the eyes of their headteachers and
through an analysis of the market data concerning school rolls. This analysis had led us to the interim conclusions set out in Chapter 3 – in short,
that the market policies were producing little evidence of increased active
choice by parents but at the same time were creating an increasingly
volatile climate within the schools. In addition the effects of marginal
changes in schools' rolls were beginning to have a much more marked
effect on the financial resources available and headteachers increasingly
felt a need to be sensitive to the image and reputation of their schools.

At this stage of the study we aimed to get deeper into the workings of
these processes within two schools in order to explore the impact of
marketization on the working lives of those employed within schools. It
was not intended that this stage of the study would provide 'representative' data which would facilitate generalization about the experience of
schoolworkers in general – either within County Town or throughout

England. Rather, our purpose was to seek illuminative data which would provide an indication of the range of possible experiences taking place in contemporary primary schools and help in our exploration of the marketization–management relationship. With this in mind, the decision about which schools to focus on for in-depth case study was a particularly important one.

We considered characteristics such as the size of schools, their religious affiliation if any, the gender composition of the workforce (particularly the heads and deputies), their location and place in the market. However, finally, in the hope that much insight could be gained from contrast and comparison we decided that the two schools should show marked differences in their attitudes – particularly the attitudes of their managers – to the policies of marketization. This after all was the focus of the study and it was most likely that the illuminative data we were seeking would arise from schools which contrasted most strongly on this dimension. It was this decision which led us to the two schools which are described below.

Both schools appeared to be running smoothly. At Hill Edge Junior School, management was characterized by an entrepreneurial approach. The head was in favour of 'breaking free' from the local education authority. The chair of governors was a self-employed business person, with three companies.

Management at the second school, Christchurch Primary, was characterized by an apparently much more traditional approach. The head spoke warmly of the LEA and the chair of governors was a former (retired) employee of the LEA.

The more detailed insights which were revealed as the schools came under closer examination through case study indicated that these differences were somewhat superficial but that some of the similarities were very superficial. In particular, early in the study of Hill Edge, it emerged that the appearance of smooth running was very deceptive. There was considerable tension in the school. However, as the two studies progressed further elements of dysfunctionalism also emerged at Christchurch. The value of the case study approach was affirmed through this process of peeling away 'layers of reality'. Insights were gained which could not have arisen at earlier stages of the project or from even broader surveys.

Case study methods

The two schools were studied over a 12-month period commencing in spring 1994. Data were gathered through a series of interviews and through attendance at a range of meetings. The headteachers were interviewed again at length and frequent brief discussions were held with them throughout the year. The deputy heads and most of the class teachers were also interviewed. When difficulties arose in one school in arranging interviews with two of the teachers, some use was made of a simple questionnaire. Interviews were also held with the school secretary in each case, and with the chairperson of the governing body. Both the interviews and the questionnaires used a common framework of areas of discussion, but the details varied according to the particular role of the interviewee.

Staff meetings were attended at both schools, as were regular meetings of the governing bodies. A parents' meeting at one of the schools, called in advance of a ballot on opting out, was observed. There was also a limited amount of classroom participant observation. We did not see this as a major part of the study because our intention throughout was principally to examine the relations between workers in the schools, rather than between adults and children.

Access to each school was readily agreed, initially through the headteacher. When teachers were interviewed it became clear in both schools that there was some lack of clarity about the reasons for our interviews. On more than one occasion it emerged that some teachers understood we were in the school as some kind of inspection or pre-inspection process. The co-operation of governors was sought by the headteacher. On attending governors' meetings, we were asked to give a brief account of the research project. We used this as an opportunity not only to indicate the broad area of interest but to give reassurance about the ethical basis of the research in terms of preserving the anonymity of individuals and the confidentiality of the data gathered. In general there was ready and whole-hearted acceptance of our presence in meetings and apparent openness and frankness in interviews. This was tempered on some occasions however, as indicated in the accounts below. We also found that teachers in particular gave two different kinds of account as time went on. The first drew on a professional discourse about policy changes in primary schools and their impact on their work. The second, which sometimes came when the tape recorder had been switched off and as a sense of trust had been built up with the interviewer, was a more personal discourse which revealed levels of disquiet which had not been apparent initially. We examine this phenomenon in more depth in Chapter 7.

Hill Edge Juniors

Located in a working-class estate on the edge of the town, this school served 7–11-year-olds. It shares its site with Hill Edge Infants, serving 4–7-year-olds. The two schools run separately in most respects, the exceptions including a shared caretaker, heating and alarm systems. One of the neighbouring primary schools was the first primary in the area to go for grant maintained status. This had not had a marked effect on Hill Edge, but the head was certainly anxious about maintaining sufficient intakes in order to sustain two-form entry. This anxiety related more to patterns of rehousing taking place within the town than to direct competition from neighbouring schools, although there were also apparently a number of children who were not transferring from the infants' school, as they might normally be expected to do.

Relations with the infants' school were far from straightforward. The head of the infants' school had been appointed during the previous year. There was apparently no move by the LEA or by either governing body towards amalgamation. This was surprising, given the proximity of the schools and the difficulties with sustaining rolls in the junior school. There appeared to be considerable animosity between the junior head and both the current infant head and her predecessor. One of the junior school governors was working in the infants' school. Another governor was also on the infants' school body.

The junior school had a two-form entry, making eight classes altogether, two for each year group. There were 8.4 teaching staff plus the head.

The headteacher was experienced, having been in post for about ten years. He was also extremely voluble, offering extended interviews, which proved challenging for the interviewers to manage. He described himself jokingly as the managing director of the school, acknowledging a major change in the nature of headship since he had started:

> I think some heads have a problem because they cannot get used to the fact that their job has changed. I mean you are no longer, for want of a better term, the sort of school's senior teacher.
>
> (Interview HT10)

At various times he was very critical of the LEA, teachers' unions and Her Majesty's Inspectorate (HMI). He thus appeared to align himself with much of the government's critical attack on 'the education establishment'. He was of the opinion that all of these bodies tended to prevent him doing what he wanted. The school's Ofsted inspection was imminent when our fieldwork finished. The head was very cynical about this process and believed it would be unfair. He felt that the inspection team was unlikely to take into account the nature of children entering the school. The press would only report any weaknesses which the inspection identified. Although he said he was not in favour of GMS ('opting out') in principle, he nevertheless saw it as the best way forward for his school. He had been applying for other headships, but they were outside this LEA, because he thought the LEA would block any local appointment.

At the beginning of the case study, with the exception of the head and the deputy head, all of the teaching staff were women. During the summer of 1994 there was considerable staff change, however. Four out of the eight full-time staff left. Those departing included the deputy head, who was appointed to a headship in a neighbouring authority. One teacher was retiring, although whether she was getting full enhancement to her pension was unclear. One was leaving teaching to train in an alternative career. The fourth was returning to her home county because she was 'homesick'.

The deputy was a sounding board for the other teachers who would sometimes visit him at home to get his support for job applications they were making. There was considerable tension between the head and the deputy; the chair of governors said they tended to compete for popularity amongst the rest of the staff. The deputy indicated that he thought the head was close to a nervous breakdown and at one time advised us to stop our research in the school. He said that the head tended to lose his temper, act unprofessionally, bully his staff and did not negotiate with them over anything. He 'punished' the deputy for 'interfering' by removing all his non-contact time.

The head suggested there was a division amongst the staff along age lines, with younger staff not sufficiently respecting older. He also thought the predominance of women was unhelpful:

Men bring humour to staff room and prevent bitchiness among women. Balance is needed, humour is needed. Women will tend to often go on about small grumbles where men will brush them away.

(Interview A17)

The four departing staff were replaced by four new teachers, all of whom were newly qualified. In other words, in September 1994, half of the teaching staff were technically completely inexperienced. Two attempts were made by the governors and head to appoint a new deputy. An appointment was not made however, with the head indicating that the field was insufficiently strong. The head had persuaded two of the experienced teachers in the school to share the responsibility of the former deputy by joining him in a three-person senior management team. These two teachers were not receiving any additional remuneration for this extra responsibility and were extremely ambivalent about taking it on. It was generally felt in the school that the staff changes had brought some relief to the previous tension. One of the two depicted the situation thus:

I think it would have been a shame to upset the present arrangement, because things are so much smoother, pleasant, the whole building is much nicer to work in and the atmosphere, and it would have been a shame. You know though at the back of my mind I must

say I do wonder if it was – if I say rigged it sounds rather wicked
doesn't it? – but you know . . .

(Interview A47)

The secretary – or 'office manager' as the head called her – played a
major part in the administration of the finances. She felt overworked and
underpaid, was not a member of a union but thought she really ought to
be.

Since 1993 the chair of governors had been a parent governor who
joined the governing body in 1992. He had two daughters at the school.
He was a self-employed accountant and an agent for TV journalists. He
became chair following a brief tenure by a Labour Party nominee who
resigned after criticism around allegations of insufficient supervision of
children during staff shortage on a sports day. The chair appeared to take
a very active approach to his responsibilities, indeed he had calculated
that he provided approximately £6000 worth of services to the school
each year, costing his time, telephone calls and correspondence. His explanation for his commitment was as follows:

I always feel that if you have got some criticisms and you want to
change the system, the democratic way of doing it is being part of
the system. . . . I feel that when people moan about things and yet
they are not prepared to help change them, they lose any right to be
listened to. I am a firm believer that if you are not prepared to 'do',
don't criticize.

(Interview G3)

The head and the chair collaborated closely, although the chair implied
major weaknesses in the head's management skills. They both indicated
that the influence of Labour Party governors was considerable, trouble-
some but fortunately poorly co-ordinated. They referred to them as 'the
politicos'. Although the chair would describe himself as non-political (or
jokingly as an anarchist) his politics were very clearly those of the 'active
and responsible citizen', of the 'self-made man'. From a working-class
background with poor educational experience himself he took the view
that it is no good 'whingeing about things', 'you should get involved'. He
was not an efficient chair of governors' meetings. They were disorderly,
the agenda was not followed and there was considerable vitriol between
some of the governors on several occasions.

During our case study the question of opting out became a key issue in
the school. The head and chair were keen on GMS because it would both
increase their funds and give them greater financial control. There were
some different views on whether the school had healthy finances or not.
Most of the staff indicated that they felt they were strapped for cash
in terms of spending on resources. However, one of the teachers had

stumbled across the published accounts of the school in the local library and read that there was a £30,000 surplus.

At a governors' meeting it was suggested that they would have to lose 1.5 teachers if the school did not opt out. However, the governors never took a vote on GMS; this was pre-empted by the submission of a parental petition, surreptitiously orchestrated by the head and chair (so the head told us), obviating the need for governors to vote at a meeting.

At the parents' meeting held as required by the legislation, opposing views were put by a LEA representative and by the head of an opted-out primary school from another part of the country. The vote ensued but was declared invalid because the school had issued one paper per family rather than per parent. On the re-run the vote went in favour of opting out and the school moved steadily towards grant maintained status.

Throughout the process the teaching staff kept a low profile, at least with parents. At the parents' meeting questions were asked about the views of teachers and governors, but the only responses given were that there was a variety of views and parents should approach governors or teachers on an individual basis. In interview the teachers generally disliked the idea of opting out, but in so far as they felt it would improve resourcing they felt it could be positive. They did not perceive any significant change in job security or conditions, having sought assurances through their unions.

This then was a school where there were a number of internal conflicts – in particular between head and staff and between governors. There were anxieties about numbers of children entering the school, about the image and reputation of the school and about the school's ability to maintain its staffing levels and management structures. It was undoubtedly an unstable institution and the move to GMS, with the concomitant 'detachment' from the LEA, was not likely to improve the working relations within the school.

Christchurch VC Primary

Christchurch was a Voluntary Controlled (Church of England) primary school with a family centre and a special needs unit. The family centre was provision for pre-school children, funded through the local authority. The special needs unit received children from across the authority with specific literacy learning difficulties, sometimes referred to as dyslexia.

The school was based on a junior school, built in the 1960s, which subsequently had an infants' department added. It served a predominantly working-class community, although there was more diversity in terms of social class and ethnicity than at Hill Edge, as one might expect in this 'quasi-inner city' environment. One teacher estimated that 50 per cent of the children lived with only one natural parent.

The head had been in post for about five years. He was generally supportive of the LEA and sympathetic to its predicament, as resources were removed and local planning became increasingly difficult. He appeared to be generally efficient and organized and, for example, ran a well-prepared INSET day reviewing the school's development plan (among other matters), which was much appreciated by the staff.

In interview he acknowledged the supportive role of the LEA and emphasized the community orientation of the school. Indeed he felt that all primary schools should be locally-oriented and that open enrolment might undermine this:

> I believe [that] in the primary phase of education the school should first and foremost serve the families in that locality, and I find it very difficult in terms of open enrolment, there is a possibility, taken to extreme, that a school could lose its identity within the community it serves . . . We have our own perceived catchment area in the locality of Christchurch, and I would never turn a child away if it came from [Christchurch district].
>
> (Interview HT7)

Apart from the head there were approximately 14 teaching staff. The deputy head was also male and had been working at the school and one of its antecedents for a considerable period (almost 25 years). The deputy was very loyal to the head, expressing great admiration for him:

> in difficult situations . . . I see my role quite simply as to provide support for the head. Because in this day and age I see heads as very beleaguered animals and it is very easy for people from parents to staff to create problems and the head seems to be a very often unsupported figure.
>
> (Interview DH1)

However it emerged that amongst some of the other staff there was a serious lack of confidence in the deputy. The head of the infants' department, for example, who played a significant though apparently not very well-defined managerial role, such as preparing papers for staff meetings, and managing school meals staff, felt that she took on a lot of responsibilities which might be properly expected of the deputy. It also emerged that the head himself had some anxieties about the deputy. This emerged only gradually through odd comments and actions. The head, for example, joined the interview which was taking place with the deputy and attempted to check what had been said with interviewers afterwards.

There was one other male teacher, who took a long term secondment from autumn 1994 to work with a child counselling scheme. All the other teaching staff were women. One junior teacher was a particularly forceful member of staff and apparently popular with others, although she had no formal management position. There were some indications of staff difficulties over the previous two years but these had not yet become very open. Nevertheless, like Hill Edge, Christchurch was losing a significant number of teachers by the end of 1994, two from the infants and one from the juniors.

As the case study went on, it became increasingly difficult to gain access to staff for interviews. Appointments and arrangements were broken, often apparently through non-communication. Eventually two of the staff were asked to fill in a brief questionnaire as an alternative to taking part in a face-to-face interview. It was difficult to ascertain the reason for these barriers, although we speculated on a number of possible causes. Again the school was approaching its Ofsted inspection and this became increasingly a matter of concern for the head and the staff. But the research team sensed there was more to it than this. Teachers can be very discreet when necessary.

Being a VC school, the governing body included church representation. The chair of governors was a retired architect who had worked for the LEA and was married to a retired headteacher. He ran governors' meetings in a strictly procedural manner. The deputy head was the elected teacher governor.

The chair of governors was opposed to many of the recent changes in school governance. He was particularly scathing about the tendering for services such as cleaning and building. Drawing on his own field he indicated anxiety that the use of local independent architects, while it might save schools money in the short term, could lead to an increase in design errors and faults which could be avoided when specialist local authority architects were used. He was also concerned about the need for accountancy skills among headteachers (who had been 'trained to teach and look after educational standards of their school') and about the increasing workload on unpaid governors.

Opting out was also discussed by this governing body, as required by law on an annual basis. At a meeting in March 1994 the following discussion was recorded:

> Governor wants to hear both sides. Another suggests as situation is evolving it may be time to reconsider. (Last year they dismissed it out of hand.) Vicar is concerned to see how much money will come to the school. Believes when 75 per cent have opted out then LEA will go and everyone will be forced to opt out. Chair is concerned that the debate will end up as a political discussion which he wants to avoid.
>
> (Field notes G5)

At a subsequent meeting an official from the Diocesan Education Office made a presentation to the governors, which was effectively a statement of the Church's general opposition to GMS. There was no dissent from the view presented, although one or two questions were put about the possibility of other local schools opting out and thereby changing the nature of the local market. This school did not have any problems with its enrolment numbers.

In fact, the head had worked out that, by opting out, the school could gain by £185,000 over three years, but: 'What I believe in and what I could get for these children are two different things' (Interview HT7). The deputy head's opposition was based on his Christian commitment: 'I think GMS . . . is enticing people to pare another little slice off somebody else's slice of cake' (Interview DH1).

The school had become locally managed at an early stage. It emerged that there was a considerable degree of entrepreneurial activity, which meant that the overall finances of the school were extremely healthy. The LEA-supported initiatives, that is the family centre and the special needs unit, certainly did not create a drain on the budget; if anything they created a surplus. There had been speculation when open enrolment and LMS were first introduced that specializing in special education might be seen as threatening to the reputation of a school and thereby lead to the loss of numbers (e.g. Whitty and Menter 1991). This had certainly not been the case here. Indeed, the school had bought its own minibus and this was used to collect the children for the special unit from around the town. The LEA paid the school for this service, which might otherwise have been undertaken by a private transport company. It was also possible for other schools to rent the minibus, at a competitive rate.

The other interesting enterprise undertaken by the school was the use of its grounds as a parking space on Saturdays when major teams were visiting the sports ground opposite the school. It was said that approximately £1000 had been raised during the previous season. The head undertook his turn at staffing this car park with the school's parents' organization.

Christchurch then was a school in which some of the traditional values of primary education were firmly espoused by senior staff. However, here too there was evidence of some of the marketizing forces creating an element of instability in the school. The governors were beginning to show signs of uncertainty and there were weaknesses in the staffing and management structure which were more exposed in the new world of school planning and explicit management.

Comparison

A varying degree on inherent instability was thus identified within two case study primary schools. On the surface the schools present a public image of efficient and well-organized educational provision. However, the experience of new forms of management, often revealed through expressions of great personal stress, distrust of colleagues and deep cynicism about the benefits of educational reform led to the conclusion that there may have been an underlying crisis of management within both schools. This was certainly more apparent at Hill Edge than at Christchurch (where it was perhaps incipient rather than manifest), but three key common factors support the view that both schools were affected.

Firstly, there was a high degree of alienation among the workforce in both schools. This was clearest among the teachers. There were two elements to this. One was the disenchantment with the nature of their work. The holistic and humanistic view of primary education which had brought them into this work had been eroded by bureaucratization and intensification. They no longer felt fulfilled in their relationships with children in the classroom.

> The pressure has increased tremendously. It is not the class work. The thing that really struck me, the first two years of teaching you had so much time with the kids you didn't have all these other peripheral (. . .) assessment or working out budgets or things like that. Maybe it is because I didn't have so much responsibility then. But I feel in the last five years things have just been building up more and more and more. And the actual teaching in the class is nothing compared to what school life is all about.
>
> (Interview A46, Hill Edge)

Such views were common in both schools.

This cynicism extended to the inspection process:

> [Inspection is] just one of the one hit wonders. It doesn't matter how good you are, you are going to be criticized anyway, so I am not too bothered really. I know I will be very nervous the actual week.
>
> (Interview A63, Hill Edge)

The overall effect is one of feeling devalued. One teacher, with seven years' experience, talking about assessment said:

> we are trying to make the assessment as useful as possible, but it's just all the other stuff really. You are having to justify yourself all the time. You are never trusted to do anything.
>
> (Interview B48, Christchurch)

The other element was the degree of tension between staff. The amount of factionalism and outright hostility had increased dramatically. These twin factors had undoubtedly played a large part in some of the departures of staff, either to other schools or out of the profession.

Secondly, the influence of grant maintained status was felt in both schools. While it had been a source of disenchantment and division in Hill Edge, in one sense it had been a unifying force at Christchurch. The governors and teachers had been drawn together through their common opposition to it. Nevertheless the anxiety about the potential effect on school resources of not opting out was beginning to be felt. If and when an increasing number of primary schools opted out this anxiety was likely to increase, and in a school which was already engaged in a considerable amount of entrepreneurial activity, it seemed unlikely that the pressure could be resisted for long.

Thirdly, although the changed financial regime had less immediate impact on the day-to-day lives of teachers, the underlying tendencies arising from local management and open enrolment had had a serious impact on the institutional cultures of the schools. Management's major current priority was maintaining the financial health of the school rather than developing the quality of educational provision. The government's argument is of course that the two are directly related through parental choice. On the ground though there is little apparent connection between the two.

Conclusion

The two schools examined above were selected because on the face of it they had very different responses to the marketization of primary education. However, as we have seen, closer analysis reveals great similarities.

From relatively small-scale qualitative work of this kind it would be rash to draw conclusions which are over-generalized. However, the indications which emerged from the initial analysis of our larger sample of 12 schools in the town were generally consistent, as are patterns of change identified within the eight LEA sample of the PACE study (Pollard *et al.* 1994; Black 1996). It is thus our view that such dysfunctionalism of the kind we found in these two schools is likely to be connected to the management of marketized primary schooling.

This is not to say that there were no benefits to be gained from any of the reforms in primary education. Certainly, there was widespread recognition by the teachers in our study of the benefits which had accrued from collaborative planning based on a common (national) curriculum, which had created greater continuity and greater guarantee of progression for pupils. But it must be asked at what cost this has been achieved.

The extent to which these features are entirely attributable to post-1988 policy is an important and difficult question to answer. There is no doubt that many primary schools had elements of dysfunctionalism in the pre-ERA days. But in reading accounts of life in these schools (including ethnographic studies and quantitative surveys) those elements often related to what were perceived as personality clashes between teachers or, if they were related to structural inequalities, they were generally a reflection of structural features of the society as a whole. Such features of course persist to this day, but have been exacerbated by specific market policies targeted at the education system.

There has been a tendency within the study of quasi-markets to concentrate on economic indicators such as choice and allocation of resources (see Le Grand and Bartlett 1993; Bartlett *et al.* 1994, for example). In education this tendency is reflected in a common emphasis on the 'structural' rather than 'process' elements of educational policy. While not ignoring such 'structural' factors, these case studies have sought to provide a fuller account of the impact of marketization by exploring changes in culture and social relations within one set of institutions experiencing marketization. They have demonstrated the destructive impact of these policies on working lives and relationships in two primary schools. The commodification of primary education through marketization appears to have wreaked considerable damage to human relations.

These findings suggest that there has been a significant change in the culture of primary schools which goes well beyond the educational process taking place in classrooms. The 'culture of collaboration' depicted, for example, by Nias *et al.* (1989) has been eroded and replaced by a culture of uncertainty and alienation.

Gender relations in both schools were particularly interesting. The heads and deputy heads in both schools were male and the great majority of other staff were female. This is not an uncommon feature of primary schools. The increasing business orientation of primary school management may be seen to entrench yet further the traditionally paternalistic nature of primary school headship (an aspect to be explored in more depth in Chapter 6).

The analysis of these two schools, taken together with the wider picture presented in the previous chapter, enables us to move forward to a deeper analysis of the changing nature of management and workplace relations in primary education in the next two chapters.

6   THEMES IN THE CONTROL OF WORK

Introduction

In this chapter we focus on changes in work definition and work processes, and on the formal and informal operation of controls, with particular attention to the role of the headteachers and the governors in our two case study schools, with additional data from the wider sample of headteachers. The significance of financial controls is very strong. New relationships with the LEA and the possibility of becoming grant maintained ('opting out') have had a powerful influence on the way heads see their world.

In studies conducted in the pre-reform era the headteacher was seen as the educational leader of the school, but did not necessarily seek to bring about particular pedagogical approaches. The extent to which the curriculum was planned across the whole school varied quite widely. Resources and staffing, admissions and transfers were coordinated by the local education authority. The role of governing bodies was largely advisory. These practices may be described as 'the old management' of primary schools.

However, the fact that earlier studies of primary school management did not indicate that headteachers wielded considerable power and control over schools' staff may be more an indication of the research methodologies which were employed than of the actual situation. The majority of studies failed to examine the common-sense notion of harmonious work relations that accompanied the cosy 'familial' image of the English primary school. Even those studies which did take a critical approach to the purposes of primary schools and to the role which they could play in social differentiation (e.g. Sharp and Green 1975) failed to give the same critical attention to work relations within schools.

Grace (1995) does note the paradox that the very creation of the egalitarian spirit of educational leadership in the 1960s and 1970s could only occur through the power of the headteacher in the first place:

in most cases, the introduction of a more democratic and consulta-
tive style of school leadership depended in the first instance upon
an exercise of hierarchical initiative by the headteacher.

(Grace 1995: 194)

In other words (although Grace does not put it in this way), the structural
inequality has been continuous. The hierarchy, patriarchy and author-
itarianism which had emerged with the development of state schooling
had different manifestations at different periods in the history of
schooling.

So we would argue that the hierarchical power within the staffing of
primary schools has become more exposed since 1988. It was perhaps
always present in latent form, but the managerial imperatives introduced
through the Education Reform Act (and subsequently) have brought
about its overt enactment. That is not to say that the exercise of power in
primary schools takes the same form as it did before the apparent liberal-
ization of the 60s and 70s. As we have argued earlier, the new discourses
which have characterized post-Fordist management across Western societies have their place in education too – indeed, they have a particular
resonance in primary schools, as we shall see.

Since the 1988 Act, primary school headteachers have had to cope not
only with enormous curricular and assessment innovation, but with a raft
of new management and governance policies. These have included the
devolution of financial control, new powers and responsibilities for governors, open enrolment and the possibility of becoming grant maintained.
Furthermore, the introduction of whole school planning, appraisal and, in
some places, local bargaining and performance-related pay, indicate a
shift in the nature of staff management and labour relations in schools.
All these changes – these multiple innovations (Wallace 1992) – could be
described collectively as bringing about a 'new management' in primary
education, replacing the frequently paternalistic, unfocused and implicit
practices of the old.

The government's claim is that the introduction of measures such as
these will lead to the improvement of educational 'standards'. The introduction of competitive practices, in short the marketization of (primary)
education, should improve the 'performance' of schools. But as Ball (1990)
has pointed out, these changes bring with them a shift in the functioning
of schools towards a business culture: 'The model of organisation which
the ERA implies is clear: it is that of governors as Board of Directors and
headteacher as Chief Executive' (Ball 1990: 67).

There is contemporary evidence of a severe reduction in the autonomy
of class teachers (Pollard et al. 1994), which can be understood as a de-
skilling or proletarianization of teachers (albeit with elements of 're-
skilling') (see Lawn and Ozga 1981; Grace 1987; Ozga and Lawn 1988).

We look at these issues in depth in the next chapter. What we intend to consider here is the nature of changes in the work of headteachers, in order to understand the relationship between the work of these two occupational groups.

Like class teachers, headteachers have had little choice about whether to implement curricular and assessment innovations. But in addition they have been faced with the range of changes in the governance and management of schools outlined above. New skills have been called for and the nature of headteachers' work has changed at least as much as that of class teachers. The de-skilling of class teachers has required headteachers to become more directive in their management and more reliant on indicators of performance. The self-concept of the primary headteacher has had to shift from that of educational leader/paternalist/community servant to that of manager/salesperson of an educational commodity.

Changes in heads' work were detected early on during the implementation of the 1988 policies (see Hellawell 1991; Jones and Hayes 1991). In her case study of a primary school, Acker (1990) found that the headteacher concerned felt increasingly pressurized during this period of transition:

> What Mrs Clarke [the head] feared was that some of her greatest satisfactions in the job were being crowded out as the managerial side took priority, notably her occasional chances to teach in the classroom, which provided a way to keep in touch with the children and gave credibility with the teachers.
>
> (Acker 1990: 268)

Acker found that reassuring the staff was becoming a very prominent part of the head's role.

Webb's study of the implementation of the National Curriculum at Key Stage 2 (in Burgess *et al.* 1994; see also Webb and Vulliamy 1996) also found that heads expressed the need for time for counselling their staff. Furthermore, her research indicates that the question of a head's credibility with his/her staff has taken on a new dimension since the implementation of the Act. She found that such were the demands of LMS and non-curriculum-related management, that heads were not even able to maintain a sufficient level of knowledge to play a full part in curriculum development and planning, let alone to make a significant teaching contribution.

> In medium and large schools . . . [m]any headteachers considered that they did not have the same knowledge of the [National Curriculum] Orders as their staff nor the same confidence and experience in teaching the new aspects of some subjects. This both reduced their credibility and their ability to provide curriculum leadership . . .
>
> (Burgess *et al.* 1994: 43)

Similar views are expressed by the six British headteachers whose accounts are presented by Mortimore and Mortimore (1991).

The 'PACE' project interviewed 48 primary sector heads in 1990 and again in 1992, 1994 and 1995 (Pollard et al. 1994; Black 1996). Amongst their early findings was that heads perceived staff development as one of the areas of greatest change. The most problematic area created by the legislation was perceived to arise from LMS. However, while one quarter of the sample welcomed LMS, slightly more than a quarter found it most unwelcome. The PACE team have found, on the basis of four rounds of interviews with heads, that there has been a continuing change towards more directive approaches which compromise 'collaborative collegiality'. The proportion of heads reporting deteriorating relationships with their staff had doubled between 1990 and 1994 (Black 1996).

Headteachers in the PACE sample saw themselves as being maximally exposed to new legal requirements, management responsibilities for curriculum, staff and finance and new accountability procedures. However, although the inspection threat loomed in many of their thoughts, their commitment to pupils and the idea of staff collegiality meant that they actively sought to face external pressures and, in some sense, to protect staff from them. This, of course, reflects something of the ideological commitment to personal relationships which, as we saw in the introduction to this chapter, has been an established part of primary school cultures for many years (Nias et al. 1989). However, headteachers did still make many new requirements of their teachers and other staff.

Regarding teachers, PACE data shows how they in turn sought to mediate external demands and those arising from the headteacher, again much under the influence of their professional ideologies and commitment to the quality of children's classroom experience (Pollard et al. 1994; Broadfoot and Pollard 1996). Thus they judged the extent and form in which new subject content, specified in the National Curriculum, was to be introduced; they mediated the use of standardized assessment procedures to avoid pupil anxiety; they interpreted the new roles which they were allocated, for instance as curriculum coordinators, and they sought to protect the quality of their relationship with pupils.

For the pupils, the result of such successive mediation was relative continuity in classroom experience, but then, if you have always been relatively powerless, being powerless under a different type of regime is not such a big change.

Of course, such a centre–periphery model, with layers of mediation and interpretation as a government policy moves to the point of implementation, could also be extended to incorporate the role of local education authorities and, in different ways, governors and parents. At each level too, we must not forget that mediation of impositions from the layer above is only part of the story: additional initiatives, pressures or requirements may also be generated whether independently or deriving from other sources. Agency remains important even in contexts of relative constraint.

The overall picture then is one of complexity in change – but with certain patterns of strategic response, often reflecting the influence of pre-existing ideologies, being detectable.

As is inevitable in a period of rapid, successive change, perceptions of major problems have changed over the years, as new innovations have been laid upon old. In the mid-1990s it is likely that headteachers' prime concern will be with the new procedures for school inspection which have been introduced.

Headteachers' perspectives and responses to marketization

We turn now to examine the responses of the headteachers from our sample of 12 primary schools. They were asked about their role as managers and about their perceptions of 'the market'.

Market exposure through open enrolment

Our examination of the history of admissions to the 12 schools (and others) indicated that there was very little active choice being made by parents (see Chapter 3). The number of children on roll was steady or rising in the majority of schools. In the 33 city schools 18 per cent were experiencing rising rolls, 76 per cent were maintaining their annual intake and 6 per cent were experiencing falling rolls.

Of the 12 heads we interviewed only one had experienced any change as a direct result of open enrolment, a policy which had been implemented for over a year when the interviews took place. In that school, the roll had increased. Only one headteacher saw parents of the school as 'clients', the others felt this was an inappropriate term to describe them. The majority of heads believed that rather than choosing freely between schools, enrolment patterns reflected the old fixed catchment areas with minimal competition between them.

In those schools where enrolments were below the standard numbers, heads believed this was to do with local demographic change or the construction of new schools. (A school's standard number is the designated pupil capacity of a school – that is, it sets the limit for open enrolment.) All the headteachers supported open enrolment in principle but none thought that it could work in practice under the current arrangements. The reasons given for this were lack of spaces at the popular schools. The new schools were attracting parents but they were full and had waiting lists, therefore parents could not place children in their first choice school. Nine of the heads expressed disappointment that the parents' expectations had been raised and felt that their school should cater primarily for the children in their locality.

We identified a particular concern felt by primary schools where their standard admission number did not translate easily into whole classes. Heads felt that mixed age classes were unpopular with parents and, with the introduction of the National Curriculum, increasingly difficult for teachers to plan for. However, if their standard admission number was, for example, 40, then this was too large for one class and yet not large enough for two and would mean mixed age classes. It was the headteachers whose intakes were not multiples of viable class sizes who were concerned about enrolment. The situation was made worse in small schools as small intakes afforded no flexibility. Primary schools were at a disadvantage to secondary schools in dealing with this difficulty, for where an optimum primary class size of between 25 to 30, for example, would have a margin of flexibility of 1 to 5 children, in a six-class intake of a secondary school the same margin of flexibility would be between 1 to 30 children.

All heads felt able to describe the factors they felt affected parents in their selection of a school. The majority, nine out of twelve, felt that parents wanted their children to go to a school near to their home. They believed that parents found out about the reputation of schools from their neighbours and friends and that this also influenced their decision. The reputation could relate to a number of factors, including standards of academic performance, social class composition of the pupils or pupil behaviour within the school. The third factor mentioned was the physical environment. More than half the heads felt that parents were attracted to new schools because they presented a bright, cheerful and aesthetically pleasing environment. The existing roll of parents supported the heads' view that parents were choosing the school nearest to their home with the exception of the newly built schools. Each school had a few exceptional families who, for varying reasons, brought their children to the school from further away.

Each school had a small number of additional features which the headteachers felt might influence parents, though only marginally. These included family centres for pre-school children, religious ethos, infant transfer and class size.

Heads of four schools thought they were in some competition with other nearby schools. Only one saw this as outright competition. The others, most of whom had no shortage of applications from parents, were concerned at the potential damage of competition.

To summarize so far, there was little or no evidence that schools were actually being damaged by competitive market forces. Nevertheless, it emerged that a considerable amount of marketing activity was going on.

Nine of the twelve said that they had carried out activities which were designed to attract parents to the school. Of the three that did not, two felt that they had no need to do so and the third felt strongly that resources should not be wasted in this way.

There was great variety in the activities that heads described. Most of them aimed to build a good reputation for the school in the community. Those that were mentioned most often were: keeping in touch with the local press for coverage of school events; welcoming parents into the school for parents' evenings, to help in classrooms, to a special parents' room or to shows and assemblies; a good-quality school prospectus and regular letters home, and maintaining a pleasant, aesthetically pleasing environment.

So heads were willing to act to some degree as if a truly competitive market existed. They seem to have done this because they were anxious about competition or because they were legally obliged to (in the case of the preparation of a school prospectus). They were aware that the likely benefits in terms of attracting more children and hence protecting or improving the school's budget were small. Overall then there was evidence of growing anxiety about the impact of competition. The effect of this appeared to have brought about internal changes as well as increased concern with the external image of the school in the community.

The changing role of the local education authority

There was considerable consensus about the changing role of the local education authority, both about the fact of a significant change and in the evaluation of the impact of that change. All of the heads indicated that they had received good or excellent support from the LEA over recent years. In some cases this relationship was personal as well as professional: 'quite a lot of people who I regard not only as officers of the authority but as friends of the school, and in some cases personal friends of mine' (Interview HT12, Crescent Primary).

They were disappointed in the reduced level of support which was currently being offered and expected that even this level would be reduced. They referred to a voucher system which was operating to regulate the level of support which they could receive annually from the 'professional development consultancy service': 'The days of direction from the LEA are seemingly gone. They don't tell us what to do, they advise the governors what to do' (Interview HT8, Alma Road Primary).

Nevertheless there was a feeling among some that the efficiency of the LEA had improved recently: 'Obviously there are the statutory services that the LEA still provides and I think provides far more efficiently now than they did a few years ago. Legal advice and financial advice, insurance things like that' (Interview HT7, Christchurch Primary). One head, though, was quite cynical about the improvement of the reduced service: 'It is well intentioned, I think in fairness it always has been. It is trying to be even more well intentioned now because their jobs are on the line' (Interview HT10, Hill Edge Junior).

Local financial management

The requirement that schools should take responsibility for, and administer, financial matters is relatively new, for formerly these services were provided by local education authorities.

The headteacher of Hill Edge in fact acknowledged explicitly that his school was now 'a business', and this acknowledgement was presented in a jocular manner when he was asked to confirm that he now described himself as the 'managing director':

> Well, a slightly silly cliché, but in a sense, from a somewhat realistic point of view really, and I think some heads have a problem because they cannot get used to the fact that their job has changed. I mean you are no longer, for the want of a better term, the sort of school's senior teacher.
>
> (Interview HT10, Hill Edge Junior)

This same head had recently given up any curriculum subject leadership responsibility.

The heads all indicated the increased significance of financial planning and management, and some indicated that they received a lot of support in this area from secretarial staff. The 'managing director' of Hill Edge, when asked about the clerical staffing in his school, replied that the school has:

> One office manager, which is an interesting statement, who is on the highest grade but doesn't quite work full-time. And then we have another assistant secretary who works ten hours a week. The office manager really being our nearest equivalent to a bursar.
>
> (Interview HT10, Hill Edge Junior)

It may be noted that both heads who said that their (female) secretary knew more about day-to-day financial affairs than they did were men. (Compare this account with the views of the secretaries reported in Chapter 7.)

The major concern with respect to budgets was staffing levels. Age profiles had become significant and in the three cases where a school was in the process of significant expansion, new staff tended to be newly qualified rather than experienced.

There was no doubt in the heads' minds that central government was to blame for the financial difficulties being encountered. As one headteacher put it:

I have had a £10,000 cut because of this capping thing from the government, but I am convinced, I have gone into it very deeply, and I am convinced that the fault lies with the government. It is not the LEA, it is government who just assess a county town on a very mean level compared to Oxford. I've rung up schools in Oxford and Wiltshire and I have found out what they get and it is much more generous than us.

(Interview HT2, Warburton Primary)

This county has a particularly interesting recent history in respect of its relationship with central government. Political control of the county council was hung and the parliamentary representation of the area was largely Conservative. The government consistently accused the county of being profligate, a charge which was strenuously denied by all local politicians. Nevertheless the county was subject to rate and then community charge capping. This appears to have been a key factor in the large number of secondary schools in the area which opted out or were in the process of doing so (see below for a further discussion of opting out).

Management structures

The internal management structures in the schools had all been developed in response to the new demands being made on them. However, there was considerable variation in responses and this seemed to be related to the size of school. One or two schools had senior management teams, previously a feature only of secondary schools, but most had some form of sub-grouping, either on an age phase basis or on a curriculum basis, again an unusual arrangement in the days before 1988. For instance:

We have lower school, heads of department, middle school and upper school. I have a deputy head who has overall curriculum responsibility for the school and we also have a staff development officer for the school . . . And all of those people, whether it be of an administrative nature or of a curriculum nature, also have devolved financial responsibility. So we finance areas of the curriculum, we finance the day-to-day consumable aspects of the curriculum as well.

(Interview HT8, Alma Road Primary)

One headteacher actually referred to a management theorist (Charles Handy) in his explanation:

We have adopted the sort of spider web management system. He is one of the top management theorists – he started in industry but has

shifted over to education. [I am/we are] using his industrial management schemes.

(Interview HT10, Hill Edge Junior)

In smaller schools the notion of a sub-group sometimes became a pair:

Well, I suppose [it is] my deputy and myself for the juniors, and
myself and the reception teacher for the infants.

(Interview HT7, Christchurch Primary)

All of the heads referred to a range of meetings which were held in
their schools. Several differentiated between meetings dealing with 'nitty
gritty issues' and those dealing with curricular or development planning.

We have two staff meetings a week. One is to cover the general day-
to-day running of the school, the diary the planning, the events. . . .
Then on Mondays we have what you could call a curriculum meeting when we review policies or initiate a policy. We will look at the
school development plan, we have also had time given to looking at
computer programmes and personal development, we have people
in say to talk to staff on stress management, on their own self-
esteem. It is a time when I make sure it is a social time as well, I
provide sort of tea and cakes and we have a few moments when I
also ask them to give me some idea of what has gone well for them
in their last week. Infant teachers are very good at running themselves down, maybe that's because it's largely female, that they also
need a time to consciously tell people of their successes and things
that have gone well.

(Interview HT4, Wrighton Junior)

This extract is a cogent exposition of the old and the new – the need to
deal with such recent innovations as development plans at the same time
as fostering a harmonious if paternalistic culture. The use of phrases such
as 'personal development' and 'stress management' exemplifies the accommodation between the old and the new.

There was common acknowledgement of the way in which meetings
had changed.

[We have a meeting] every Thursday, with a regular very meat-
filled meeting. Nothing is allowed to fester, things come out. When
you think about it – have you ever taught? – in [town where head
worked previously] we had a staff meeting once a term, incredible,
they got away with murder. And Tuesday afternoon the head
would swan off to the Rotary and we wouldn't see him again until
the next day. He was a nice bloke and he was a fairly good head,
you know, but I would have been bored out of my head, I think.

(Interview HT2, Warburton Primary)

All of the heads had drawn up development plans. Although advice from the LEA was that plans should cover three years, a number of heads indicated that only an annual cycle was realistic. For example:

> I try to do three-year plans but I don't find them successful at all because so much happens in the space of twelve months that you have got to revise it all again, so for the present year, it is just a twelve-month plan and I shall construct another one, August, September, for the next twelve months.
>
> (Interview HT7, Christchurch Primary)

With respect to development plans, heads also had different approaches to authorship, involvement and consultation, from those who saw it as simplest to do it themselves and persuade the staff and governors that it was right, to those who sought a more interactive, developmental and participatory approach.

The new rights of governors and parents

The views of headteachers about the roles of their governing bodies varied from one extreme to the other:

> *Int:* Are they [the governors] very involved with the school?
> *HT:* Yes, it varies, some are extremely involved, others not very involved at all, but generally speaking it's a very supportive governing body.
> *Int:* What do you feel about the responsibility governors are given, are you happy with it?
> *HT:* Yes, because I work very closely with my governors. I'm quite happy. I've always had a policy of working very closely with the governing body
>
> (Interview HT8, Crescent Primary)

On the other hand:

> *HT:* [under breath] Prats! The chairman is good, he is the councillor for the area – very supportive but doesn't interfere. The two community governors, I really have to get behind, because they always leave it to me. They all work; they've got jobs. You can't expect too much. The government has been too optimistic – too much responsibility in the hands of amateurs. More responsible adults go for the large secondary schools. However some are OK. I worry about the pay structures. It will cause a lot of ill will . . . some of the governors will think the teachers are grossly overpaid. It's going to set teachers against teachers, headteacher against teacher, headteacher against governors.

> You can't have complete amateurs assessing people's pay.
> Here, who knows what will happen – I'm glad I won't be here
> when it happens.
>
> (Interview HT8, Alma Road Primary)

This was one of four heads in the sample who were anticipating imminent retirement.

Most of the schools' governing bodies had up to four sub-committees,
but one head appeared to be moving in the opposite direction:

> I have cut down on blooming committees I will tell you that. I can't
> stand waffle and time-wasting and there was a lot of that when I
> arrived. . . . You see the head's job now, as I see it, there is one way
> of keeping yourself sane and keeping it all on a rational, reasonable
> level. If you can work with your chair of governors you can solve a
> lot of problems. That building out there, you can bet your bottom
> dollar before I arrived, they would have had three sub-committees
> to talk about everything to do with it. I said to the chair of governors
> 'Look, it's my idea, I will carry the can if anything goes wrong, I
> don't want any committees, I'm doing it myself'. And that is what
> we presented to the governors. . . . I know where the school is
> going. If I make a cock-up, OK, I carry the can. But you could have a
> committee, the way the government wants it, for everything. I could
> be here until midnight every night with committees.
>
> (Interview HT2, Warburton Primary)

The involvement of parents in schools was not universal nor was there
a common mode of involvement. There was some evidence though that
parents were seen as a resource which was ameliorating the effect of a
general scarcity of resources. The strongest example of this was at Warburton Primary:

> We don't just have them listening to little Johnny read, we give them
> on-site training, particularly for our reading scheme. We give the
> parents targets to hit with the children, not necessarily National
> Curriculum, but that gives an idea. My head of infants [name],
> actually gives them some tuition as to what we are after . . . Rather
> than say off you go for twenty minutes. . . . And we get some really
> high calibre mums. Really good.
>
> (Interview HT2)

Such 'high calibre' parents were not always available:

> We have got an unemployed former pupil with a computer degree
> who can't find a permanent job. But in an area like this it is difficult
> to get the right parents. Because it seems to me anyway that the
> parents we have with any wherewithal find themselves a job, which

they have to do now to keep the family, and those that haven't got a job are those you don't want in school anyway.

(Interview HT6, Warren Park Primary)

The views of the governors themselves made an interesting comparison. In Chapter 4 we described the contrasting ideologies of the chairpersons at our two case study schools. The Hill Edge chair was a self-employed businessman whose approach to the school was characterized by a spirit of entrepreneurialism. At Christchurch VC on the other hand, the chair was a retired local government employee, who bemoaned the removal of LEA expertise from a wide range of management services. Both chairpersons were committed to a form of public service, they were both exemplars of 'active citizenship'. Both cases also showed aspects of the new balance between headteachers and governors. Without doubt the governing body of the 1990s is more significant in the day-to-day lives of heads and teachers in primary schools. If the relationship is not good then there can be considerable difficulties in a school. However, the extent to which the formal powers of governors represent genuine accountability of a school staff (especially the head) to the local community or even to a school's parents is highly questionable. The new authority of the governors (largely removed as it were from the LEA) appears to be mainly symbolic. The political balance between the head and the chair of governors can be significant, however. Major changes are likely to come about where ideologies are shared and the two can work together – this is not necessarily an open process and lacks the democratic checks and balances inherent in LEA control. School governing bodies (although not appointed by central government) demonstrate many of the features of quangos.

Grant maintained status

The first thing to be said about GMS is that it is relatively rare for primary schools to opt out. In fact, by July 1994 only 336 English primary schools had opted out, from the total of almost 20,000 schools, and the number applying to do so was decreasing rapidly. However, the county in which our case study schools were located was one of the counties in which the GMS initiative had taken hold. A high proportion of the secondary schools had opted out (29 out of the 42 schools at the end of our fieldwork), and during the period of our study one of our case study schools decided to apply to do the same.

The policy is having a considerable effect on the perceptions and practices of heads and governors of schools. While the grant maintained option still entails clear financial benefits for schools it is not surprising that some will give it serious consideration, particularly when faced with budget cuts which may lead to the loss of teaching posts. Even where heads and governors are ideologically opposed (as at Christchurch, see Chapter 4), the policy is creating anxiety and uncertainty. There is undoubtedly sometimes a domino effect – when one or two schools in an area opt out, there may be a rush for others to do so. This appears to be what happened with the secondary schools in this county. The attraction is not always a financial one, however. At Hill Edge, the school finances were perfectly healthy (with a £30,000 surplus), but the head felt so alienated from the local authority and the chair of governors was such a business-oriented person, that the two of them were strongly attracted to the idea of greater managerial autonomy.

Discussion

> HT: I like being in classrooms. I'm the old-fashioned headteacher. Today you only have to be an administrator and all this nonsense, I'm afraid I grew up in the era when you were expected to teach and be a head.
>
> (Interview HT9, Hill Edge Infants)

This head has now retired. Her nostalgic view of a golden age of headship in itself demonstrates the fact that there has been considerable change from head as educational leader to head as business administrator.

The role of primary headteachers has been changing rapidly since the wave of legislation which commenced in the late 1980s. The impact has been seen in the way in which they talk about their work and in the practices which they describe. Heads associate much of this change with their sense of an external market, though of course it would be simplistic to imply that these parallel developments in management and market ideology are *necessarily* entirely interdependent. There were, for instance, other important marketizing influences. Of these, the most significant in the mid-1990s is undoubtedly the inspection regulations which were introduced by the government following the Education (Schools) Act of 1992. These provide for inspection of all schools every four years, with publication of a report and the threat of being named as a 'failing school'. There has been considerable media coverage of the results of such inspections and headteachers have become very aware of their significance.

The old management of primary schools, with its emphasis on teams and collaboration, demonstrates some of the features of new thinking in management generally. Although Human Resource Management (HRM) is constituted by a broad variety of ideas and practices, one of its accepted features is the notion that job designs are based on teamwork and 'responsible autonomy', rather than on an explicit division of labour. It is thus not surprising that HRM is having some impact in education, where the workers aspire to democracy and collegiality. 'Responsible autonomy' is understood in industrial relations terms as a management strategy to achieve compliance through internalized norms and controls (see Storey 1989). The heads who talk about democratic decision-making, empowerment, teamwork and the avoidance of hierarchies are using some of the language of HRM. The references to industrial management practices, training schemes and enterprise initiatives such as Investment in People are also indicative of a new managerialism. The extent to which such practices create more democratic institutions, whether for workers (including teachers) or consumers (parents/children) is highly questionable. There is a strong argument which suggests that such practices amount to a more sophisticated form of surveillance and control than the old style of management. Hatcher argues that 'the overall thrust of the new managerial professionalism is to strengthen the position of headteachers *against* school governors and over classroom teachers' (Hatcher 1994: 59).

In industry such practices have been replacing hierarchical, Fordist management practices. In primary schools, on the other hand, they are replacing or perhaps supplanting implicit, paternalistic, largely non-hierarchical management practices.

The headteachers in our study were reluctant to articulate any major changes in their commitments to the children and to the staff. Some of their discourse remained traditional, particularly with respect to education and children. Nevertheless, their management practices, in some cases at least, demonstrated elements of HRM. Are these heads hanging on to previous practice and simply 'incorporating' the new discourse? Some of course are getting out of the profession and none of these expressed regret at their future retirement.

How are these changes in the work practices of heads affecting the experience of teachers and other staff? We have prima facie evidence of changes in the work relations of secretaries. What though of teachers? In the next chapter we look at this in more depth.

The study by Bowe and Ball (1992) of changes in secondary schools suggests that such is the complexity of contemporary change in schools that even the new managerialism cannot be expected to be entirely effective. The relatively small size of primary schools as organizations may be seen to reduce the degree of complexity of management. But, as with the wide-ranging curriculum responsibilities which are vested in each primary teacher, so the headteacher too necessarily bears direct responsibility for a wide range of administrative and managerial functions. One of the heads in Bowe and Ball's study off-loaded almost all of the day-to-day dealing with financial management to a deputy head. This possibility is not open to primary heads, given the normal teaching commitments of deputies. In another school in Bowe and Ball's study a bursar carried these responsibilities. Here, as we have seen in some of the County Town primary schools, there is some possibility of a similar approach. We have seen that some schools are already exploiting the 'over-qualification' of their secretaries to undertake responsibility for financial management and the development of IT systems within the school. Few primary school governing bodies are likely to decide to employ an appropriately qualified person for this role at the appropriate salary.

Our conclusion from this analysis of headteachers' perceptions of their roles is that there clearly have been and continue to be significant changes in their experiences and working practices. However, it is too simple to refer to 'the new primary headteacher'. Each head demonstrates a particular set of responses which comprise a mixture of old and new. The connections between business models of management and heads' practices are also complex, because of the close connection between these business models and some features of traditional primary school management.

Even where (post-) modern discourse and practices are more evident, the centrality of the headteacher's role in the management of the school is as clear as ever. Legally the governing bodies of schools bear a greatly increased responsibility. The perception of the heads themselves, who after all are themselves legally more accountable to those governing bodies than before, is that there is no doubt who carries the bulk of the day-to-day responsibility. It is indeed headteachers who are still carrying the can.

7

CHANGES IN SCHOOLWORK

Introduction

In this chapter we attempt to pull together and illustrate the emerging picture of management–workforce relations in the context of the primary marketplace in County Town. In Chapter 3 we set the scene, and in Chapter 6 we set out some of our observations of the complex responses of primary managers to their changing roles in a marketized context. It is evident that headteachers bear a greater burden of responsibility as they meet the pressures of accountability, higher standards of performance, and diminishing resource. It is also apparent from our data that the introduction of new managerial forms and processes sits uncomfortably on top of old, established work practices. Furthermore, it could be argued that these processes are likely to exacerbate dysfunctional tendencies within the social relations of schoolwork.

In order to explore these issues we turned our attention to the school staff. We approached the task in a theorized way, looking for specific sets of indicators that might help us in our attempt to 'read' change in primary schoolwork, rather than simply document it.

We were assisted in our research design by models of data collection that had been applied in collecting evidence about the response of workers in business and industry to the new managerial discourses of HRM. Figure 7.1 sets out those indicators of enhanced managerialism that we used as the organizational basis for this stage in our data collection.

As well as making use of our extensive data derived from interviews with the headteachers, we used these organizing concepts to gather data from school teaching staff and from school secretaries, using intensive data collection techniques in the case study schools, Christchurch and Hill Edge. Interviews and observations focusing on seven teachers and two secretaries identify the effects of the deregulation of their terms of employment and the increased control by the headteachers and

Major indicators

Increased control: horizontal rather than vertical and including the growth of group-based work.

Delegation of responsibility.

Increased measurement of performance against performance indicators and other institutional objectives.

Areas of investigation of workforce perceptions of managerialism

- Job design (definition of role, priorities, autonomy, performance indicators).
- Supervisory responsibility (location and any changes in work practices).
- Interaction with management (nature of relationship).
- Union activity (perception, significance).
- Job security (labour market position, mobility, career progression, professionalism).
- Demarcation (labour market position *viz-à-viz* other employees, sharing of responsibilities, supervision).
- Morale (levels of stress, job satisfaction).

Figure 7.1   Indicators of enhanced managerialism
Source: Adapted from Scott (1994)

governors. We argue that changes which appear to enhance teachers' professionalism by increasing their responsibilities and the opportunities for greater cooperation with colleagues, for example, the introduction of the National Curriculum, have in fact led to an erosion of teacher autonomy and resulted in demoralization.

A similar critical interpretation of the position of the secretaries is also possible, as their regrading had not brought the hoped-for recognition, either professional or financial, for their new responsibilities. In addition, measures introduced to provide greater public accountability within the marketization framework, although supported in principle by the teachers and secretaries, were overburdening schools with administration. The older teachers in particular were seriously demoralized by their weaker position, and budget cuts threatened them with career stagnation, as movement between schools becomes increasingly difficult for experienced women teachers. Their experiences reflected the conflicts in teachers' work identified by Nias (1989):

> Some of the mutually incompatible preoccupations which teachers therefore experience enter the classroom with them, the product of their own social and educational experience and their professional beliefs and aspirations.
>
> (Nias 1989: 193)

Observation of the teachers during weekly visits, informal discussions with all staff, observation of staff meetings, governors' meetings and semi-structured interviews with a representative sample of seven teachers from the two schools sought to document the experiences of the class teachers in their current position within a context of increased marketization.

The focus on the teachers followed from the arguments set out in Chapter 4 that the context of marketization would lead to enhanced managerialism (see Figure 7.1), with particular attention to:

• the delegation of responsibility
• increased control (horizontal rather than vertical), including group-based activity
• the increased measurement of performance against institutional objectives and performance indicators.

In both schools there was evidence that these features had increased and were having a serious impact on the working lives of the teachers. The changes were increasingly affecting the teachers' working lives by continually encroaching on areas which had originally been their sole responsibility, but which were now being removed from individual control and/or subjected to management scrutiny.

The teachers' responses to this encroachment on their classroom activity were presented in two very different accounts of their views of the changes, one 'public', the other private. At first, teachers attempted in a public role to present the changes in their work as positively as possible; however, very different accounts of the impact and implementation of the changes were disclosed when the teachers spoke confidentially about their private perceptions of the changes. The two versions were in conflict with each other, causing stress and demoralization. This equivocation is examined further below and in Chapter 8. The dual accounts are compared to the experiences of teachers in a situation of 'burnout', as Freedman (1988) describes the complex situation which can lead teachers to 'lash out in angry denial'.

Their experiences were similar to those identified nationally in the PACE study (Pollard *et al.* 1994), where teachers were found to be pressurized to change in ways they would not have chosen, and where changes resulted in:

> an intensification of workload and a loss of job satisfaction . . . there were increasing perceptions of a loss of autonomy and fulfilment in teaching . . . teachers were feeling more controlled and less autonomous.
>
> (Pollard *et al.* 1994: 99)

The main areas which remained under their control identified by the seven teachers were the teaching styles they used and their relationships with their children. Their response to change had not been to replace entirely the old practices with new but to continue the old and the new side by side, with the inevitable increased work-load. In this respect the practices of the case study teachers reflected the findings of the study of teachers by Campbell and Neill (1994a) (see also Osborn 1996), where despite teachers' conscientious efforts to make reforms work, relatively little curriculum change had occurred. Teachers appeared to be attempting to isolate areas of their work where they felt they remained in control.

The differences between their public and private views of their responsibilities were particularly evident in their explanations of the purposes of the changes that were being introduced. They reflected the conflict which existed between the constant support teachers were required to give to the management view of changes and their private understanding, often cynical, of the reality of the motives behind the management decisions. These tensions, both in their practices and their perceptions of management motivation inevitably affected the teachers' attitudes towards teaching as a profession and their confidence regarding future prospects. The tensions also reflected the dilemmas identified by Nias (1989), and faced by the teachers in her study:

> dilemmas which they face stem from views expressed directly or indirectly . . . Either way, teachers' inevitable inability to fully satisfy their own consciences and their wider audiences leaves them feeling simultaneously under pressure, guilty and inadequate.
>
> (Nias 1989: 193)

However, the teachers in our case study had moved on from this position to expressing anger and frustration at their position. These responses are discussed in the final part of this chapter.

Delegation of responsibility

In both schools the seven teachers had been given more responsibility in the form of extra duties. In the main these related to two areas; all had been given one or more areas of the curriculum to manage on behalf of the school, and three had been given an increased role in the overall management of the school by the creation of senior management teams. The secretaries in both schools now took much greater responsibility for financial management because of LMS, and for administration because of the introduction of computers for the school budget and pupil and staff records.

The teachers' first description of their new role presented an account of welcomed increased responsibility, which enhanced their professional role and career prospects. However, as they discussed their new roles and as their confidence in the researcher grew they wanted to provide a different version of events, identifying frustration with under-resourcing, anxiety over loss of LEA support, dismay at budget cuts and resignation at having to step in to cover the failings of more senior staff.

Additionally, the curriculum and assessment changes introduced had provided conflicts similar to those identified by Freedman (1988), between what they wanted for the children in their classes and the way they were now expected to work. Here they were given more professional responsibilities and yet were as a result losing much of their autonomy. These conflicts are examined in the context of their roles as curriculum coordinators and as members of senior management teams.

All the teachers in the two schools had been given responsibility for an area of the curriculum. In general this responsibility required that the teacher write and update policy documentation and organize and manage resources. Budgeting of resources had been restricted in one school to the senior managers and in the other to the head teacher assisted by the school secretary, now interestingly referred to as bursar, despite still being employed as a secretary grade three.

> Joan, the secretary, she is another person you negotiate budgets with. Sometimes probably more than [the head] really. . . . I think she is more aware of what is there, because she uses the computer and she knows how difficult it is to get things out of certain things. . . . She is more aware of what is going on. And also a lot of it is hidden from the class teacher's eyes. We don't fully understand.
> (Teacher interview, A46 Hill Edge Junior)

In Hill Edge the effect of the new computing facilities had considerably increased the control that the secretary held over the expenditure on resourcing. The class teachers revealed that it was in fact the secretary who decided whether a particular purchase could be made, whether or not they had been given permission by the head.

Although financial management dominated the changes that the secretaries in both schools were experiencing, there were other effects of marketization. In Christchurch, the headteacher was concerned to standardize procedures throughout the school. He had worked closely with the secretary to devise procedures for her role as school receptionist. Foyer facilities (compare with the account of 'foyerisation' in Gewirtz *et al.* 1995) had been provided to accommodate these procedures. There was a seating area for visitors and a switchboard arrangement for informing the head of arrivals.

The other responsibilities included:

- Management of 13 per cent of the schools' budgets now a 'cheque book' accounting system had been introduced.

- The introduction of a new computer system to process all pupil records, staff pay, and personnel records.
- Management of schools' funds; tuck shop; Family Centre funding; Dyslexia Centre funding.
- County Hall paper work, e.g. employment contracts; weekly absences; school lettings; invoicing for hirings.

These had all increased in complexity because of the diminishing role of the LEA. In both schools the secretaries felt that the introduction of the new computer facilities had added considerably to their workload. Both had had to attend training to upgrade their skills. However, neither felt that their new skills were rewarded.

For the teachers in both schools the introduction of ten subjects within the National Curriculum had meant that broad descriptors such as 'topic' to cover a range of subjects had now become inadequate to ensure the management of the specific requirements for each subject. The sharing out of ten curriculum subjects in schools of less than ten teachers inevitably created difficulties. These were increased by the requirement to monitor cross-curricular themes and processes, including assessment, equal opportunities, economic awareness, health and sex education, which meant that even the teachers of the larger of the two case study schools had to assume responsibility for more than one subject.

The teachers' reward for the extra responsibilities consisted of the allocation of points on the new standard scale for teachers, which reflected the earlier systems of the A–E incentive allowances. Four of the teachers described the allocation of points in terms of the old incentive allowances. None of the teachers interviewed had been awarded points for excellence of performance or for recruitment or retention purposes as the extra responsibilities required more work, particularly of the supervisory nature described by Ozga and Lawn (1988). In fact the points not only appeared to reflect the curriculum responsibilities taken by the teachers but appeared to reflect their length of teaching experience within the school, despite being described as given for a particular responsibility. It was therefore possible to find the following range within the allocation of points held by the teachers interviewed.

0 points A young teacher in her second year of teaching with shared responsibility for the school art policy.

(Interview B49, Christchurch)

An older teacher with seven years' teaching experience but in her first term with the school, taking responsibility for equal opportunities and religious education.

(Interview B50, Christchurch)

1 point A young teacher in her fifth year of teaching, a member of a senior management team as a replacement for the position of

deputy head; taking responsibility additionally for geography and music.

(Interview A46, Hill Edge)

A young teacher in her seventh year of teaching with responsibility for assessment; moderation; the school portfolio; history and geography.

(Interview B48, Christchurch)

2 points   A teacher in her twentieth year, a member of a senior management team as a replacement for the position of deputy head; additionally taking responsibility for English and health education. There had been no alternative but to award two points as her original scale allowance had been awarded when the system required that such awards were permanent. It was therefore now protected.

(Interview A47, Hill Edge)

A teacher in her ninth year responsible for a nursery department and a member of a senior management team which included a deputy head. She took responsibility for budgeting; resources; staff appointment and management; students and work placements; liaison with the infant department; liaison with social services; adult education classes within the unit; pre-school curriculum requirements. Her points were also protected because of a previous award.

(Interview B33, Christchurch)

A teacher in her eleventh year responsible for an infant department and a member of a senior management team which included a deputy head. She took responsibility for timetables, work schedules and absences; management of non-teaching staff; dinner time supervision; students; YTS work experience placements; servicing staff meetings; reporting and curriculum requirements. Her points were similarly protected.

(Interview B36, Christchurch)

The maximum number of points allocated was restricted by the number set by the school governors. The maximum allowed for extra staffing under the new provisions is five for extra responsibilities with a maximum of three for excellence and a further two for recruitment and retention. The maximum found in either school was two points awarded for curriculum responsibility.

In both schools senior management teams had been created. In one this was to replace the deputy head when he moved to take up a headship. In the other the head teacher had decided on a team in order to compensate for a deputy head whom he felt was not able to cope with the duties required of him. In the school where the deputy had not been replaced this was not with the approval of the staff members, who were now being asked to take on the responsibilities of the deputy head for no extra points. They believed that it was not possible for them to receive extra points for the work until after the first term and then the points would be on a temporary basis.

Although the changes to the responsibilities taken by both teachers and secretaries gave the impression of a flattened management hierarchy they did little in either school to reduce the autocracy of the head. This was more so at Hill Edge than at Christchurch. In the many interviews with the head at Hill Edge, managing the school was always spoken of in terms of a personal isolated responsibility with only a little support from the governors.

> Teachers' views may vary because their perspective is from the classroom. They may not appreciate what the head has to do.
> (Interview with headteacher A17, Hill Edge Junior)

The deputy head during the previous year had commented 'the female members of staff [*all* the other staff] are patronized, insulted and shouted at' (Interview with deputy head A34, Hill Edge Junior).

The two women in the senior management team which replaced the deputy head in this school responded differently to their new role. The younger one, who was applying for deputy headships, saw it as an opportunity to improve her CV whereas the older teacher, who had taken the role of acting deputy before, was less satisfied. She was relieving the head of the more trivial aspects of his work such as opening and sorting the post; the real decisions remained with him.

In Christchurch it was also two women who had joined the senior management team with a male head. Here though there was also a male deputy whom they were supporting. Both believed that although they worked very hard the real control lay with the head. The head of the nursery department explained how it was the head whom she approached when there were any problems (Interview B33), and the head of the infant department referred to the support she gave the head: 'he needs all the help he can get' (Interview B36).

It was noticeable in both schools that the senior management teams had enormous workloads with little or no non-contact time. The two teachers in Hill Edge received no official non-contact time at all; they had created a small break during swimming which was supported by the head. In the second school the head of infants supervised lunches every day and had given up her office to be used as a special needs room. Her non-contact time was achieved when students took her class. Teachers in both schools had experienced increased workloads, which reflected the findings of the Campbell and Neill (1994a) study where teachers:

reported significant increases in the amount of time they had to spend on work and nearly all saw the extent of such increases as unmanageable and unreasonable.

(Campbell and Neill 1994a: 71)

As a result teachers in our study were also under considerable stress. Despite this all the class teachers acting within senior management teams also remained committed to delivering exemplary classroom practice and spoke of the needs of the children. Their new duties had not changed the tasks they undertook with their classes but had grossly added to them. Their behaviour was similar to that identified by Campbell and Neill (1994a), where teachers felt they were 'victims of their own conscientiousness'. Teachers already working very long hours did not try to reduce them:

not even in the last year of it, that is 1992–93 when official acknowledgement of the impossibility of what was being asked of them was published.

(Campbell and Neill 1994a: 20)

Increased control (horizontal rather than vertical) including group activity

The most noticeable change in the reduction of a hierarchical structure of control had come about with the move from a line of responsibility from class teacher through head of department to head, to the introduction of curriculum planning groups. This move also reflected the external position of the school, where the changes in the hierarchical nature of the control and accountability had been brought about by the legislated demise of the local educational authority through such policy initiatives as local management of schools, grant maintained status, and the introduction of a national curriculum. For the secretaries, their role in the past had involved close contact and support from the local education officers. They now feared the loss of these support services and felt that they were becoming increasingly vulnerable.

With the teachers it was the introduction of the national curriculum that had prompted the introduction of peer group planning. This form of self-regulation was described positively by the teachers in terms of more collaborative working, greater curriculum continuity, greater consistency of experience for pupils and again an enhancement of their professional role through the increased responsibility.

However, the negative aspects of their perceptions of the new responsibilities were expressed as, again, an increased workload, a reduction in the professional judgements they were now required to make independently, and a belief that unnecessary changes were a result of a government view that they were no longer to be trusted. These points emerged as teachers spoke of their changing patterns of work.

The secretaries expressed similar concerns. Initially they had hoped that the increased responsibility to be taken by the headteachers and the school governors would lead to greater reward for the contribution that they made to the school. Unfortunately they realized that this was not to be the case and were demoralized. Neither belonged to a union but had, however, given serious consideration to joining UNISON. They were taking an interest in UNISON activities but admitted that it was very unlikely that they would join. They were both full-time and working alongside part-time general assistants who also helped with secretarial duties, but they felt isolated in the school. Both commented that their position as women working for male heads possibly aggravated their position.

All seven teachers spoke of the threat to their independence. That they lived with the continual anxiety of loss of autonomy was not surprising (Lawn and Ozga 1986; Grace 1987). Nias (1989) reported that nearly a third of the teachers in her early survey of the impact of the 1986 and 1988 Education Acts experienced anxieties relating to the threat to teachers' autonomy. In her study, teachers feared the threat of schools' amalgamation, local authority staffing and curricular policies, parental interference and fears of increasing centralization in the education system (which had been realized by the time of our study). Deciding on the curriculum had been central to their autonomy in the classroom. These planning and recording procedures reduced the traditional autonomy of the classroom teachers (Nias 1989), obliging them to work in teams. The head of infants felt concerned that she had lost her title of head of infants, she was now a coordinator: 'I was appointed as Infant coordinator with a measly allowance. Not head. Coordinator is the correct description' (Interview B36, Christchurch).

As with the delegated duties discussed above, these procedures did not replace activities such as individual teacher preparation but added to them. All the teachers interviewed expressed dissatisfaction with the meetings that they were now required to attend and with the administrative activities which were now obligatory, such as the recording and reporting of pupil progress through the national curriculum.

> The job's not what it was when I came into the profession I think there is so much admin. Really you can spend such a lot of time bogged down with recording things on this form and then putting a similar thing on another form.
>
> (Interview B36, Christchurch)

The meetings being attended by the two teachers of Hill Edge included:

- a weekly whole staff meeting
- a weekly planning meeting with a fellow year group teacher

- a weekly policy review meeting (the subjects were being taken in sequence)
- a weekly meeting with the headteacher
- a weekly meeting with each other.

(Interviews A47 and A46, Hill Edge)

These meetings had replaced a more relaxed system:

> We tended to meet if we felt we needed to and very often we didn't need to, although . . . you obviously worked to your planning folder, you did tend to go your own way.

(Interview A47, Hill Edge)

In the second school a similar series of meetings existed:

- a weekly whole school staff meeting
- a weekly department (infant/junior/nursery) meeting
- a weekly year group meeting.

(Interview B49, Christchurch)

For members of the senior management team these were supplemented by team meetings and governor meetings.

In both schools three meetings took place at the end of a school day, each week. The meetings had become necessary to cope with the introduction and continuing coordination of the national curriculum and the accompanying assessment, recording and reporting arrangements. In the last year both schools were facing Ofsted inspections, which had generated yet more preparation and coordination.

> There have definitely been changes. The pressure has increased tremendously. It is not the class work. The thing that really struck me, the first two years of teaching you had so much time with the kids you didn't have all these other peripheral . . . assessment or working out budgets or things like that. Maybe it is because I didn't have so much responsibility then. But I feel in the last five years things have just been building up more and more and more. And the actual teaching in the class is nothing compared to what school life is all about.

(Interview A46, Hill Edge)

The meetings dealt mostly with content of the curriculum rather than its delivery, therefore the teachers of both schools still retained a certain amount of autonomy.

> I find that in the classroom it is left to me to use whatever teaching strategy that I feel the children need – or the best way that I feel I can get things across to them.

(Interview B49, Christchurch)

However, the greatest change was the moving of the control of terms of employment to the head and governors from the local education authority. Teachers in both schools felt as a consequence there had been a move towards the employment of less expensive teachers. In Hill Edge, despite an underspend in one year of over £30,000, four newly qualified teachers had been appointed to replace experienced staff who had left. The post of deputy was replaced by the senior management team (discussed above) from staff within the school. The teachers had no doubt that this was to reduce expenditure.

The teachers recognized the effect that this was beginning to have on the movement of teachers between schools, on future promotion prospects and the possibility of taking child care breaks.

> It might be quite hard [a career break for children] . . . I think if you are older, if you want to go back to work and you are experienced, I don't think you should always be taken on a temporary contract. . . . It's not very good and heads are having to look for cheaper options. So they are having to look for probationers. So it is quite hard if you are the top of the scale.
>
> (Interview B48, Christchurch)

The movement of control to the head from the LEA was further illustrated by the decision by the headteacher at Hill Edge to apply for grant maintained status. The teachers realized the extent of their impotence in this situation. This teacher's account was corroborated by another member of staff and the deputy head:

Int: Were the staff against GM, do you know?

I think so, I think on the whole we were. We did feel as well that we were getting a lot of pro GM information and not the anti information. . . .

It does concern me and I do wonder what would happen should there be a change of government. . . .

I can only see the benefits as cash which I don't think is right. It doesn't seem educationally sound to me, to be doing something just for the money. I may have the whole scheme wrong, but that is how it feels to me. And I did have the feeling that most members of staff felt the same.

We were concerned as a staff about having nobody to, if you like, to fall back on, nobody to bail you out. . . . As you know, the governors in theory employ you. And if you disagree with your employers, it could be a clash of personalities, who do you go to?

(Interview A47, Hill Edge)

This increased control by the headteacher was evident in both schools, and was felt at all levels. Their accounts reflected those elsewhere (Nias 1989; Wallace 1992; Campbell and Neill 1994a, 1994b; Pollard *et al.* 1994) of the pressures of increased legislation, administrative duties, prescribed curriculum and collaborative working. Ironically, this appeared to be the effect of initiatives from a central government whose rhetoric of choice and diversity suggested the opposite intention (STRB 1993, 1994).

Objectives and the use of performance indicators

The introduction of a range of performance indicators for different areas included the National Curriculum attainment targets, the assessment regulations, the publication of league tables, the requirements to produce an institutional development plan, the Ofsted pre-inspection information, appraisal, financial targets and the standard admission numbers. Together they were creating a need for the excessive amount of planning, coordination and administration that was continually observed.

The teachers' public and positive account of these changes was that they were introduced to ensure accountability to the public and in particular to parents as customers or clients of the school. They were also part of an attempt to provide national consistency and a standardization of educational provision. These were all moves which the teachers felt able to support in principle. However, the negative aspects were presented by the teachers as an introduction of overburdening administration and a reduction and waste of teaching time, which had led to a lowering of standards because topics were dealt with more superficially than before, 'reducing the quality not the quantity of service provided' (Apple 1988).

This was also the finding in the study by Campbell and Neill (1994a), where teachers thought that the National Curriculum had lowered standards in six of the 12 subjects that they taught. In the PACE national sample the teachers supported the national curriculum but also believed it threatened the fulfilment of their basic commitment to the learning and development of young children (Pollard *et al.* 1994).

Their experiences matched Apple's account of the conditions which led to intensification:

> Thus this new generation of techniques – from systematic integration of testing, behavioural goals and curriculum, competency based instruction and prepackaged curricula to management by objectives, and so forth – has not sprung out of nowhere, but has grown out of the failures, partial successes, and resistances that accompanied the earlier approaches to control.
>
> (Apple 1988: 105)

The teachers in the study, however, did not continue to try and subvert the changes. Their positive accounts of the opportunity the initiatives provided for greater accountability and standardization were genuinely supported and spoken of as an enhancement of their role. Is this an example of the 'misrecognition' which Apple refers to or a genuine enhancement of their professional role?

In both schools the objectives which overwhelmingly preoccupied the headteachers were in relation to their budget projections and have been discussed in Chapter 6. The way these financial targets impacted on the position of the class teachers in the school has already been referred to above in relation to the restrictions placed on their mobility and the resourcing of the curriculum areas for which they were responsible. There were, however, other objectives central to the management of the school which also increasingly affected the work of the class teachers and schools' secretaries.

The headteachers of both schools recognized the requirement to have institutional development plans, although only one of them had in fact drawn one up. In this school the plan had been shared with the staff at staff meetings and had formed the basis for an in-service day. In the other school the plan had never been constructed. The deputy head, concerned at this, had offered to write one but had been prevented from doing so by the head.

> DH feels HT is unable to cope with Ofsted inspection, does not have
> SDP and seems unlikely to face up to the work that has to be done.
> (Notes taken during interview DH6, Hill Edge)

In interviews the head claimed that the plan existed. However, the failure to produce a plan was confirmed by the two members of the senior management team who replaced the deputy. They were now preparing for the Ofsted inspection and realized one would have to be produced.

> What is a development plan? I don't know whether one is in the
> process of being written at the moment.
> (Interview A46, Hill Edge)

> Well Mr Thorpe is drawing up the development plan so we haven't
> actually seen that one yet.
> (Interview A47, Hill Edge)

In Christchurch, in addition to the school development plan, they had adopted a curriculum planning system, published by another LEA, and in one department were also involved with the Investors in People scheme to review their staff development plans.

The National Curriculum and the national assessment requirements had produced targets and goals for the teachers to meet within their classrooms. The planning and coordination that was required for these initiatives has been discussed above. Both schools had rigorous weekly, fortnightly and termly forecasts. It was interesting that although all the teachers complained of the increased workloads they all welcomed the introduction of a National Curriculum. They held the reservations about the curriculum which had been expressed nationally and had therefore welcomed the Dearing review.

> I think it is slightly better than it was, because of Dearing. I think people feel a great weight is about to be lifted from them in some way. People still feel very frustrated – I feel very frustrated by the amount of paper work.
>
> (Interview B48, Christchurch)

At an individual staff level it was the introduction of appraisal that had created targets for the teachers to work towards. This was a new initiative in each school and had had variable results.

In Hill Edge the two teachers interviewed had both been involved with appraisal, one as an appraiser. Although they had both been apprehensive, the appraisal interviews had been enjoyed. For the younger teacher who was appraised targets had been set for her development within her school role and to a certain extent for her career development. The interview had led to her attendance on a course in order to develop the curriculum area for which she was responsible, and time to develop her mathematics skills. The interview had also identified her lack of early years experience, but this had not been followed up.

The older teacher had not been appraised and she felt that she no longer had career plans:

> I think I have got to the stage now when I haven't actually got any career plans, which sounds a bit awful I know.
>
> And because I feel that the job really is so much different to what it used to be, I do get worn out by it at times. You know I really welcome the holidays, and I am having to work at weekends more and more.
>
> (Interview A47, Hill Edge)

This teacher confided that she had once considered being a deputy or head but had abandoned such plans. She was now 47 and intended to stay in her present position until she could retire at 55. She appeared to reflect the anxieties of the teachers in the study by Nias (1989), where it was the fear of stagnation rather than the lack of reward that created concern: 'For these teachers diminished career prospects appeared to relate much more closely to an expressed dread of professional stagnation than they did to material incentive' (Nias 1989: 125).

The lack of recognition for experienced classroom teachers has been identified as an inherent weakness of the new pay structure even by the School Teachers Review Body, who suggest it is a major factor in explaining withdrawal from teaching (STRB 1994).

In Christchurch the situation was similar: the younger teacher had been appraised and as a result had been given more responsibility, in this case, for assessment in the school. The two older teachers had acted as appraisers but had not been appraised themselves. Neither felt that they were likely to develop their careers further.

Teacher morale

For the class teachers and school secretaries within the two case study schools the changes in school management had led to increased responsibilities, particularly for curriculum areas, but this had not been accompanied by a reduction in the autocracy of the headteachers. Structurally there had been a flattening of the traditional hierarchy of management posts with the creation of senior management teams in both schools, and with the removal of the post of deputy head in one and the posts of head of department in the other.

Both the class teachers and secretaries, however, felt that they were in a weaker position as they had lost the employment protection of the local education authority, and in one school this was threatened further by the anticipated move towards grant maintained status. The teachers' position was also weakened by the threat of budget cuts, which made their experience unaffordable and of no real worth when compared to the savings achieved by the appointment of newly qualified teachers.

Appraisal of the teachers and the regrading of the secretaries had not even begun to address the stagnation of career development felt by female senior staff, who despite displaying senior management skills and each having more than a decade remaining in the profession felt that there were no prospects of moving on to other positions.

These changes had created for the class teachers a situation where they questioned their wisdom in choosing teaching. Three of them would no longer recommend teaching as a profession to their daughters. The two younger teachers felt they had not chosen wisely.

> I wasn't prepared for the amount of work and the amount of time, and the amount of energy and the feeling of being drained, and trying to be cheerful with 25 children demanding your attention.
>
> (Interview B49)

> I shall probably go out of teaching . . . There are other areas that I
> am interested in as well. Sometimes I don't think it's healthy to be a
> teacher at times.
>
> (Interview B48)

The older teachers had all decided on compromises which amounted almost to leading a dual existence. We realized in some of the interviews that the version we were being given was a public version of the events and conditions of their experiences as class teachers. Once the tape was switched off and trust had been established we were able to hear a different version of the events, which explained many of the remarks which were recorded but only hinted at different situations.

The most striking was the cynical interpretation which the four women who were members of senior management teams gave to their new position. They all saw their new roles as requiring them to perform duties which they were not adequately rewarded for. In Hill Edge they both saw their position as a means of saving money, with the added benefit for the head that they would relieve him of trivial activities such as sorting the post, and at the same time get him off the hook by preparing for the Ofsted inspection. Between them they were writing or updating every policy statement in the school. The secretary of Hill Edge could no longer contain her dissatisfaction with the changes and therefore expressed her concerns openly to staff and visitors to the school alike.

In Christchurch the two women were covering for an incompetent deputy head (a man), and although they felt their management responsibilities contributed enormously to the running of the school they felt this was not acknowledged by the head or governors, who took their extra workload for granted.

In the first school the two teachers led the interview towards the fact that they had discovered there had been an underspend in the budget of £30,000 or more by visiting the local library. They had originally taken the same position as the headteacher and spoken of a tight budget which had meant staffing levels were threatened. After the interviews both teachers explained how angry they had been when they learnt of the true financial position. They believed the head had been lying in order to ensure the school would move towards grant maintained status.

In contrast to the way they described their senior management roles the teachers spoke positively but almost apologetically about their teaching. They regretted the way in which the new policies reduced the time they could spend with the children in their classes. It was the work they did directly with the children that produced the job satisfaction.

> Job satisfaction comes from self-achievement and the response of
> the children, and parents occasionally. No one else ever tells you
> you are doing well.
>
> (Interview B50)

Conclusion

The material above provides some interesting connections to our over-arching concerns in making sense of changes in primary teachers' work. It also provides some material on the work experiences of other school staff members, conventionally known as 'support staff'. The data lend support to our general critical interpretation of trends in work, as, in the case of the secretaries, it is clearly a long way from Saran and Busher's (1995) exhortation to incorporate such staff into collaborative cultures.

The case of the teachers, and the disjuncture between the public and private accounts, is also interesting in the light that it throws on the interpretation of research data on changes in primary teachers' work. If we are correct in our assumption that the new managerial discourses 'manufacture consent' to current changes, then it follows that articulation of criticism of such change is rendered more difficult by those same discourses. Within a framework of accountability and improved stand-ards, it is hard to find secure ground from which to speak about the loss of control over teaching, and its supplantation by administration and the apparatus of management and teamwork.

The gap between the model of the responsible, accountable profes-sional on public display, and the private experience of bitterness, anxiety and overload is also indicative of the covert coercion of the new manage-ment. It is also significant that these teachers should internalize their responses to that coercion, and thus live out the consequences of change in terms of fractured and fragmented identities. Re-professionalization as an effective team member, a good organizer and coordinator, and a skilled facilitator does not seem to be sufficient to meet the absence of traditional child-centred and teaching-oriented professional identity for these particular teachers. Perhaps their experience is unique, or uniquely difficult. Perhaps they 'misrecognize' the opportunities being offered to them. However, it could be that the tendency of researchers to find what they are looking for has resulted in an under-reporting of feelings of alienation and de-skilling, which follows from caution on the part of the teachers and an objective stance on the part of the researchers.

Gender, re-professionalization and de-professionalization

There is another aspect of these findings – and of our overall discussion – that repays attention here, and that is the way in which the issue of gender claims attention in both our analysis of the impact of the new managerialism and in our discussion of most of the research on primary teachers and their work. This is by no means to suggest that gender features largely either in conventional accounts of the management dis-courses with which we are concerned, or that it is a major theme in relevant research. On the contrary; discussion of re-professionalization takes place almost without reference to the gender composition of the workforce under consideration, and to the gender split between managers and workers. Research on primary schools, with some exceptions, pays little attention to the gendered division of labour within them.

Yet these are significant issues. We will return to them in Chapter 8, but for the moment it may be helpful to set down some of the ideas that emerge from the adoption of a gendered perspective on the experience of new management in primary schools. These include the following:

- Are women more vulnerable to the coercive/co-optive strategies inherent in the new managerialism than their male colleagues? The conscientiousness of women primary teachers (and other women workers) is well documented – does that contribute to pressure and anxiety in the face of new management strategies?
- Are women more vulnerable in terms of their traditional tendency to feelings of guilt and responsibility in the face of difficulty? Do they feel obliged to compensate for the inadequacies of others, and does their tendency to favour group work and shared responsibility (Pitner 1981; Shakeshaft 1989) actually result in a gendered distribution of work within the new management modes?
- Have researchers failed to give appropriate attention to the impact of gender on changing work in the primary school because their perspectives are themselves filtered through a gendered lens? In other words, is primary teaching work seen as relatively uncomplicated because so many of the workforce are women? Is the idea of complex reflective practitionership as the basis for autonomous professional practice and identity accorded little defence in the accounts of reform because primary teaching is seen as 'female' labour, and thus of less significance?

These are very important questions, and we shall return to them later in the book. For the moment we wish to stress that our discussion of gendered perspective adds a further and important dimension to our critical reading of managerialism. It leads us, for example, to consider whether the core and flexible teaching workforces currently emerging are divided on gender lines, and if these new regimes are extracting yet more service from their female workers. Finally we need to consider if the complex interplay of gendered understandings and behaviours is contributing to an incomplete picture of change in the primary school.

In the next chapter, we re-engage with the larger debates that frame our thinking about these, and other, related issues.

8

RESTRUCTURING WORK IN EDUCATION AND BEYOND

Introduction

In this chapter we discuss some of the findings from our comparative work in nursing homes, and return to some of our main themes concerning the ways in which we understand changes in primary teachers' work in the context of market-driven managerialism, and in the broader context of explanatory frameworks in the social sciences.

We start from the point raised in Chapter 1: that much research in education is somewhat narrowly drawn, with a tendency to see as relevant only those ideas that have been developed in the sphere of education. The challenge facing us in this chapter is to discuss some of the debates within the theoretical frameworks we have used in understanding areas of work beyond those of education and the education professions.

In doing this, we want to indicate some of the thinking that lies behind the theoretical reference points that we have selected as useful to us, and we also want to clarify our position in relation to the current debate on the nature of post-Fordist change, in order to make more explicit our very critical position taken on apparently progressive changes in work organization. Finally we want to highlight the element of continuity in this approach, in that it builds on earlier accounts of teachers' work that see teaching as labour process (Connell 1985; Ozga and Lawn 1988). This history of engagement with the labour process framework means that the narrative of control of teachers' work remains unbroken, and that post-Fordist forms may be understood as part of a pattern of control that varies in its strategic components but that is a constant source of tension and contestation within the occupational group.

In revisiting these issues we wish to re-emphasize the break we are making with so much of the research on particular professions or occupations that is confined within its own exclusive history. Long and detailed accounts have sought to find some feature or episode that could explain the trajectory of the profession under discussion (Johnson 1989). The age-old danger of functionalist accounts of change is well illustrated in this literature. In adding to the level of detailed description of a particular occupation, these studies themselves contribute to the establishment of a host of microscopic relationships which appear to contribute to the construction of causal relationships (Smith 1973).

The temptation within this paradigm is therefore to continue to collect data and information, which ultimately acquires sufficient 'volume' to offer an explanation of the relationship of one variable to another. A potential side-effect of this style of research is a lack of purchase on the causes of occupational change, the researcher remaining rooted to the intellectual spot while accumulating, through considerable research effort (and expenditure), a large and conspicuous volume of evidence.

A further undesirable side-effect of such research is that over time few connections are made between one area of social life and another. The life-work of the specialist is to dig ever deeper to unearth more data and thereby gain a fuller understanding of the specialist subject. The price of approaching research in this manner is therefore an inability to see the comparative developments elsewhere within the social system, which might shed light on the peculiar conditions pertaining to a particular occupation or industry.

By contrast, willingness to observe changes across work boundaries is likely to illuminate more fundamental and broad-ranging processes, which may well require consideration in relation to the entire working population rather than to some fraction of it. In other words, the entire labour market could be undergoing restructuring resulting from a combination of state, fiscal, and labour policies, as well as shifts between sectors of the economy resulting from international pressures.

Understanding the restructuring of a particular occupation as part of a larger process removes the danger of isolating the explanation and searching for unique historical/developmental outcomes. Seeking to establish a chain of causality within a single profession/occupation diminishes the significance of pressures at the macro level of policy-making. The focus on a single occupation exaggerates the 'particular' profession/occupation dynamic, thereby suggesting an evolutionary set of stages in development. A direct parallel with our argument can be seen in Johnson's discussion of the use of trait theory in explaining the nature of professions:

> Trait theory rarely includes any systematic treatment of the general social conditions under which professionalisation takes place. We may conclude that one of the underlying assumptions of the approach is that it is the inherent qualities of an occupational activity which autonomously determine the way in which institutional forms of control will develop – neglecting any reference to the

effects of such factors as the prior existence of powerful and entrenched occupational groups, or the extent to which governments or academic groups' institutions may impose their own definitions on the organisation of the occupation and the content of its practice.

(Johnson 1981: 14)

After more than a decade of restructuring at the level of the state, the organization and potentially the individual, recognition of the commonalities between occupations and professions in this process is overdue. In attempting a comparative basis for understanding occupational restructuring in the 1990s we have adopted a broad labour process perspective in researching the nature and impact of marketization on the process of primary school education. However, this is not an unreconstructed materialist account of labour process theory; instead it acknowledges methodological and theoretical problems.

As Thompson and McHugh suggest when discussing this approach:

> even if the resource provided by labour process theory is valuable, there are still gaps in explanations of key organisational processes. Some of this can no doubt be remedied by further research, but it is important to recognise the limits inherent in the perspective. It sets organisations specifically in the context of capitalist production, which is both its strength and its weakness.
>
> (Thompson and McHugh 1995: 42)

In an attempt to capture the historically unique developments associated with the last 15 years of restructuring and reorganization within the UK, the labour process approach can be complemented by other insights derived from the various areas of the sociology of work. These diverse traditions are united in their attempts to understand and explain developments that connect the broadest level to the individual, for example: from the level of the state, state policy formation, the sectors of industry, the resulting occupational structure, the work organization and individual experience. This necessarily eclectic area of research can supplement the labour process tradition; in particular, recent work on the social construction of work identity connects to emergent developments in both the structure and process of work organizations (Le Bier 1986; Casey 1995).

Theoretical diversity

In earlier chapters we discussed the usefulness of considering changes in the work of teachers within a theoretical framework encapsulating the following premisses:

- that there has been a major change in the organization of advanced capitalism, reflecting crisis and reformation
- that as a consequence work and production are moving from Fordist to post-Fordist forms
- that these differentiated forms are mirrored in the organization and production processes of education institutions
- that marketization drives the necessary destabilization of traditional bureaucratic professional work cultures that characterized pre-reform provision
- that managerialism becomes a key feature in securing the process of transition.

These ideas are controversial, and all are open to challenge. No single theoretical stance can be demonstrated as holding a monopoly of explanation, however we believe it is reasonable to put forward a series of related and coherent propositions that together reinforce a particular line of reasoning and build on each particular argument.

Part of the original intention of this research project was to avoid the isolationism of most orthodox educational research. Returning to this intention as we draw to a conclusion reminds us of the importance of locating changes in the schooling system within the broader changes experienced within the economic system.

In our introductory chapter we did no more than signal the significance of these contextual factors; here we revisit them in more detail, in order to reinforce the broader framework of our study.

Accumulation, crisis and markets

There can be little doubt about the existence of a crisis of accumulation experienced in most Western economies at the end of the 1960s and early 1970s. Whatever the explanation, the consequences have sent shock waves through the assumptions and practices of governments in their formulation of policy to 'manage' the economy. What has been called the period of 'managed capitalism' (Fulcher 1991) was brought to an abrupt end by the realization that the international competitiveness of the United Kingdom had fallen to an unsustainable level.

From a position where the economy had been dominated by large-scale monopolistic corporations engaging in production for mass markets (Fulcher 1991), manufacturing was required to restructure itself under the banner of rational economics to create new 'segmented' markets, which would answer more precisely the newly acquired 'needs' of the consumer.

As we indicated in Chapter 4, alongside this restructuring of industry, an equally traumatic change was taking place in labour markets, where a degree of regulation associated with a form of corporatism was dismantled partly by the sectoral changes engendered by decline within traditional industries, but also initiated by politically-inspired statutory reforms, which severely curtailed the role and significance of trade unions.

A third element in this radical shift from 'managed capitalism' to 'de-regulated capitalism' was the restructuring of the state sector, encompassing the apparent reduction of the role of the state by reducing welfare functions and redefining relationships between other spheres of the state sector, for example, education. In future education would more closely reflect the needs of the productive process and thus make a vital contribution to solving the problems of lack of competitiveness.

In response to this 'crisis' (O'Connor 1973), the state had to be restructured not only in its capacity to contain budgets and thereby attempt to control the financial crisis, but in such a way as to ensure fundamental reforms in the mode of operation. A major change was the replacement of bureaucratic procedures with 'output' measurement.

Within this climate, aided by the emergent techniques of performance management, a new impetus was given to the effective management of labour costs, as Ferner suggests:

> Constraints on expenditure have focused attention on personnel costs which constituted around two-thirds of current government consumption in most European countries at the end of the 1980s. Changing management structures have placed public managers in a different framework of incentives and responsibilities, creating new pressures for change in aspects of industrial relations and human resource management – work organisation, payment systems, bargaining levels and so on.
>
> (Ferner 1995: 22)

In attempts to gain greater control over these labour costs, private sector management techniques were seen as appropriate mechanisms for ensuring closer monitoring of the human resource in the public sector.

Human resource management (HRM), with all its panoply of techniques, was therefore a highly favoured candidate for widespread adoption in the achievement of new levels of labour control, particularly because of its closer relationship with the language of the market compared to its early form as traditional personnel management.

Of course there would be many who would take issue with HRM as a coherent set of ideas and practices (Blyton and Turnbull 1992). Originating in the US and introduced to the UK by a mixture of academics and management consultants, the debate continues around the credibility and authenticity of HRM.

Nonetheless, however it is portrayed, its continuing presence in the language of personnel practice points to the inescapable conclusion that it is effectively serving a powerful set of interests, though its application may be restricted by financial stringency. As Sisson suggests:

> Most large British companies, faced with ever intensifying international competition and scarce resources, will most probably seek what they perceive to be the benefits of the model (e.g. co-operation, commitment, flexibility etc.) and yet will be unable to incur the costs involved in implementing it in full.
>
> (Sisson 1995: 16)

There is a high degree of fit between the language of HRM and current government initiatives for education. HRM contains the potential for 'professional' co-option through the language of 'development', while simultaneously relying upon technologies of measurement which render the individual increasingly exposed to external corporate definition.

In all of these transformations, the role of the state has been formidable. No account of the changes in occupational structure could proceed without reference to the increasingly central role played by it in shaping the context and rules by which both the professions and occupations live in the 1990s.

Management, flexibility and the state

Accounting for this increasing role is a more complex task than we can undertake, even allowing for our ambitions. One line of thought suggests that capitalism itself has shifted on its axis to reveal a different set of institutional arrangements. From this point of view the particular explanations for these changes from 'managed capitalism' to 'deregulated capitalism' are diverse and range from optimistic accounts of post-industrial society, which herald considerable improvements in well-being for the majority of the population through flexibility, 'smart' working and new technology, to those more pessimistic explanations which see an extension of current trends of polarization precisely because as a consequence of new technologies and techniques, power becomes yet more unevenly distributed.

Whether these developments are seen as 'new times' (Hall 1988) or a reinvention of very 'old times', it is the case that the process of restructuring has broken down, and continues to break down, old assumptions and boundaries. Within the recent history of the UK, this has sustained a political agenda which has engineered the installation of markets within a wide range of arenas previously considered unsuitable or unsustainable for such an allocative mechanism.

In this context, as we have seen, rational economics has supplied an argument which suggests that state bureaucracies are no longer efficient at distributing resources. It argues that the paternalism and dependency implied by these old structures no longer effectively allocate and motivate. Vertical integration, which had so successfully reconciled diverse sets of activities and achieved coordination and control, was, in this reading, associated with waste, overstaffing and poor administration (Frances *et al*. 1994). Markets were seen as important mechanisms to ensure that resources were allocated more efficiently and that previously protected areas of economic activity were exposed to the disciplining affects of competition.

Privatizing 'from within' imports aspects of market relationships into organizations and generates new sets of conditions for the other 'factors' of production. How this is done, and the effects it has, form part of the puzzle that we have attempted to explore. Once again there are a series of theoretical issues which we wish to revisit at this point in order to assess the extent to which they have helped us reveal the impact of markets on such a disparate set of relations within the structure of schools. The intention here is to highlight the outline of the theoretical map which has informed much of this project, and indicate the basis of our contention that the particular labour process of teachers is subject to a form of restructuring similar to that experienced in many other related professions and occupations.

To explore some of these parallels within the project, research was conducted within County Town in related areas of work, that is in the small service providers of residential homes for the elderly and fast-food outlets, and the data from these comparative investigations will be discussed below.

Restructuring, epochs and Fordism

Much of the debate between the competing theoretical explanations of change in the nature of work lies in the contested assumption of epochal change in the development of the capitalist system. Evidence from the effects of the oil crisis of 1973 on the nature and structure of international business are used to argue for a rift in the nature of the production process which subsequently redefined patterns of consumption and fundamentally altered the role of the state in civil society (Jessop 1988).

For some, this provided evidence for a regime of production which was distinctive from the mass production associated with Ford. 'Fordism', a term coined by Gramsci with a pejorative sense, was intended to describe the dehumanized system of production based upon Taylorist principles of management and control, but the term has come to be seen as encapsulating the defining logic of the modernist period. Mass production alongside mass consumption set the contours for most Western economies (Gramsci 1971). Integral to the project of the modernist period is the abiding belief in the positivist assumptions of rational thought and logic. Taylor's system of management suitably exemplified this conviction. He was the first management writer and theorist to see how to harness the power of scientific logic to overcome opposition to his ideas. His exhaustive empiricism, reflected in his obsession for measurement, led him to argue for the 'neutrality' of his findings; he had discovered the 'laws of work'. In this sense he appealed to science as a justification for his analysis of work (Taylor 1947). This logical, rational conviction was the hallmark of this period of modernism.

A belief that Fordism was the defining feature of the modern period of capitalism has been challenged from a number of perspectives. Hyman (1991), for instance, argues that it is unrealistic to use this narrow conceptualization of a car manufacturer to define the stage of economic development: 'the notion that economic activity was once driven by mass consumer goods markets . . . is at best impressionistic' (Hyman 1991). Others like Littler (1982), Bagguley (1991) and Williams *et al.* (1992) would argue that Fordism in its own terms was not widely distributed across American industry, even within the car industry.

To reinstate Gramsci's important contribution to understanding the novel developments associated with Fordism, we need to see Fordism as developing a new level of intensification through the detailed restructuring of the organization of work. As Watkins (1994) points out, it is this hegemony enacted by the use of wider moral and cultural mechanisms which is a new departure from older forms of factory-based control. Terms like 'efficiency' and 'sound management' become part of everyday language as the workplace becomes increasingly enmeshed within the wider society.

The precise impact of this 'new' regime of production on the occupational structure of the USA stimulated Braverman to produce one of the most useful explanations of how a particular regime of control could shatter a set of assumptions underpinning an occupational structure existing in US industry at that time (Braverman 1974).

The obvious attraction of adopting the Fordist metaphor for describing a particular 'accumulation regime' (Jessop 1988) lies in the parallel that can be drawn between different sections of the labour market. The mass production tendency associated with the production of manufactured goods can easily be transposed on to other groups of workers in the public sector. Teachers can be seen as a professional group increasingly restructured into new forms of labour power. As the detailed operations of the classroom, managed through the professional (craft?) skills of the teacher, are increasingly extracted and abstracted from the classroom (Lawn and Ozga 1981; Ozga and Lawn 1988), the work of the teacher is redesigned along standard sets of procedures which, through systems like the national curriculum and testing, ensure that controls are established and the 'one best way' of teaching is increasingly built into the training and operations of new staff.

Using the idea of Fordism in this way, clear parallels can be seen between industrial, educational and many other forms of work in advanced capitalist society. Ideas of 'professional autonomy', contrasted with 'vocationalism', are challenged by this analysis; whether called a professional, a manager or a worker, the job titles cannot conceal the shared elements of increasing control and loss of autonomy. The demarcation between grades of occupation continues to socialize incumbents into a false sense of security, status and hierarchy. Socializing members into the language of a profession can in one sense be seen as part of the contradictory process (MacDonald 1995). Teachers at one moment are appealed to as independent professionals with a sense of service, whereas in their experience of work, pay and their general conditions of employment they are treated like many other groups of bureaucratically controlled workers experiencing ever-increasing amounts of routinized work associated with greater degrees of control. If they manage to retain a sense of professional purpose, then it is exercised in creating space around the routinized work. More innovative teachers might be those who can see and create the opportunities for innovation, expression and autonomy, the very features of the traditional professional role.

The Fordist account of modern capitalism captures many aspects of new patterns of work endemic to many parts of the workforce. If, however, it is used to explain an entire epoch and all aspects of that epoch it falls short, like many meta-theories. According to Gramsci, it was the novel adaptations of the productive system of Fordism that merited special attention, not its capacity to act as a technological logic to explain all elements of society. As Watkins (1994) indicates, quoting Gramsci:

> in his work Gramsci reminds us that the emergence of new forms of common sense in periods of social upheaval (as for instance, in the workplace) is not a question of starting from scratch for 'these things, in reality, are not original or novel: they represent simply the most recent phase of a long period which began with industrialism itself'.
>
> (Watkins 1994: 35)

The power of harnessing a Fordist analysis to the study of changing patterns of work lies in its demonstration of the increasing bureaucratization of work and the capacity of management and their agents to harness increasingly sophisticated technologies and techniques to engineer higher levels of coercion and consent to the point where, increasingly, control is internalized through the evermore effective socialization conducted in agencies in the wider society. Miller and Rose (1994), for example, have provided a fascinating account of the role of the Tavistock Institute in creating a form of 'therapeutic authority' to provide professionals with a new vocabulary:

> For the many professionals of the apparatus of welfare were all engaged, in one way or another, in shaping the conduct of others. The Tavi would contribute to a decisive transformation of what it meant to be 'a professional' of the conduct of human conduct.
>
> (Miller and Rose 1994: 12)

Therapeutic professionals, human resource professionals, management development professionals and many other 'experts' are increasingly concerning themselves with engaging with the subjective individual, searching out new technologies for shaping the identity of new professional workers. Hierarchical bureaucracy may well have had its day but in attempting to replace it, technologies of control appear to be emerging in often contradictory forms. We feel that it is important to acknowledge this, and to consider the extent to which our case study material provides evidence of changing forms of control, with new modes co-existing alongside earlier forms, and containing elements of contradiction.

The appearance of flatter structures and more flexible patterns of work has led to the assumption that for many professionals, devolution of responsibilities and apparent autonomy provide evidence of work being enhanced, creating opportunities for greater discretion and possibilities for greater satisfaction. As we noted in our discussion of public sector professionals in Chapter 4, it is useful to distinguish between positive and critical readings of the new regulatory modes.

Post-Fordism?

We emphasize this fluid state of transition, and the debates around interpretation of it, because it is tempting to impose an illusory order on change in so many facets of work and organization. Many social scientists see a new and different set of arrangements already in place, emanating from a new stage in the development of capitalism.

By definition, social scientists seek to identify emergent trends and developments; at the heart of the social science enterprise there is often a preoccupation with identifying 'new' societal arrangements or a search for the means to hasten a new stage into existence. In that sense 'epochs' are of special significance, providing the evidence for arguing for the possibility of change. Post-Fordism thus appears to hold the promise of another set of organizing logics on which to hang the disparate sets of structures, experiences and contradictions within the world of work. For some, this rupture with the 'old' order heralds a very different type of society and hence work itself is seen as offering greater meaning through increased levels of responsibility and the devolution of powers.

The work of Atkinson (1984) and the ensuing 'flexibility' debate, alongside Piore and Sabel's work on the 'Second Industrial Divide' (1984), interpret the new epoch of post-Fordism as a cause of optimism. A government committed to ending rigidities within labour markets and introducing markets within the public sector has been eager to amplify any evidence which might support the growth of new forms of flexibility (Pollert 1991).

Though both Piore and Sabel and Atkinson's accounts might share in a positive interpretation of the post-Fordist epoch, that is where the similarities between the two approaches end. Atkinson's model adopts a view of the future business organization reliant upon a series of 'flexible' arrangements which generally favour capital at the expense of labour. Numerical flexibility, functional flexibility and financial flexibility either independently or collectively combine to create a divided workforce, with one section sustaining a career path with all the attendant conditions of employment, while the remaining sections experience varying degrees of job insecurity and weakened career routes.

Both Atkinson and Piore and Sabel use flexibility to express forms of restructuring leading to devolution, control and responsibility, which in their view enhance the experience of work. Old bureaucratic hierarchies are dismantled and replaced with 'cooperative' patterns of work between devolved units, where individuals can benefit from the greater apparent autonomy of jobs which at times may require multi-skilled workers. At the heart of their project, Piore and Sabel seek to defend a new market for skilled workers, who will experience greater discretion in utilizing skills and new technology to achieve economic success.

Such post-Fordist accounts can once again appeal to those who see restructuring in the teaching profession as re-professionalization. With primary schools released from the 'captivity' of local authority bureaucracy, they are 'free' to get on with managing their own affairs. With budgets, greater discretion and autonomy aided by parental involvement, like those experiencing the 'second industrial divide', they can start to shape their own futures.

Though some of the initiatives associated with the moves towards flexibility contain the potential for improvements in work, such an optimistic outlook for the future of professionals and other skilled workers appears at odds with the evidence of confusion, ambivalence and stress coming from the research data on the primary schools. A theoretical framework which makes more sense of such experiences may be found in the work of the regulation school. Writers like Aglietta (1976), Boyer (1990) and Jessop (1990) all draw upon an Althusserian tradition which establishes the crisis of capitalism as the defining logic for explaining the structure and experience of work. Chapter 1 made reference to their interpretations in explaining radical changes associated with the transition from Fordist production regimes to flexible post-Fordist regimes of accumulation. Some writers (Watkins 1994) argue that a distinction should be made between post-Fordism and their particular explanation, which, through its critical stance, is better described as a neo-Fordist account in order to allow for the greater intensification of the labour process resulting in a deterioration of the experience of work.

At the heart of their analysis is an account of the interrelated institutional powers which exist to ensure the security of capitalist reproduction. It is the capacity of this set of arrangements to 'regulate' the capitalist system which forms the core of the regulationists' perspective. In this reading neo-Fordism points to the significance of new discourses aimed at co-opting workers, and identifies the technologies associated with HRM and the other new rhetorics as adjuncts of management control.

This theoretical framework which highlights the latest manifestations of control at the level of the workplace and connects this to the overall process of restructuring at the level of institutional arrangements appears to provide a logic for making sense of many of the findings associated with the research data emanating from the primary schools.

To extend the test of this theoretical utility, the discussion will turn to the subsidiary research programme which sought to make comparisons with patterns of employment within the same study area.

Commercial markets, labour and control

So far we have argued that the pattern of restructuring in primary schools has resulted in a set of experiences which differ little from those of many other professional and occupational groups within the UK labour market. As part of the research programme, a small sample of organizations within the study area which existed in very different employment settings was analysed. Fast-food outlets and residential homes for the elderly were both included in the sample.

Access to these more commercially sensitive sectors proved difficult, and in the case of the fast-food outlets it was impossible to recreate the level of detailed analysis to compare to the primary schools. Some impressionistic data was achieved but we were unable to obtain the cooperation of the owners in securing detailed interviews with staff.

In the case of the residential homes for the elderly, access was gained to the equivalent number of sites, that is, people at 10 homes were interviewed and one became a case study which resulted in several in-depth visits made over a number of weeks.

Regulation, ownership and control

Throughout the 1980s rapid expansion took place in the provision of residential homes for the elderly. The government's own projections for growth in this sector were, however, inaccurate and failed to predict the very rapid expansion in demand for such services. Within the private sector of this industry there appeared to be considerable opportunities for investment with good returns. As a consequence many new proprietors entered the market at this time with the prospect of what appeared to be a guaranteed level of return from an expanding market.

This period saw the number of beds, nationally, grow by 5.1 per cent per annum between 1980 and 1992 against economic growth of 1.8 per cent (UBS survey in Foster 1994). By 1992, the overall DSS support totalled £2.53 billion. Profit margins were substantial from the early days, further encouraging a speculative approach. With predictions of poor future demand, escalating costs and a tightening up of quality controls at the end of the 1980s, the local authority homes in the study area were becoming a liability. As a consequence of the changing levels of standards demanded, the authority at one stage was requiring standards that it was unable to meet in its own provision. Following the threat of legal action these homes were transferred into the private sector, along with many of the senior staff. A non-profit-making company was established, which supervised 23 homes of which 6 were within the study group, representing more than 50 per cent of the sample studied.

The market for these homes within the study area was therefore mixed, ranging from the large modern non-profit-making homes, to the large-scale private provider, right down to the small independent homes run as family businesses.

Management and employment in residential homes

The resulting gendered pattern of employment within the homes was almost universal in that 97 per cent of the homes in the study group employed an almost exclusively female workforce. Where men were employed they worked on the periphery as gardeners and maintenance workers. Of the 10 homes studied, staff levels ranged from 2 full-time employees to 15, but the majority of employees worked part-time and these were all women.

Rates of pay also varied but all were at very low levels. In the large non-profit sector, care workers received £4 per hour; in the small private homes this fell to just under £2 per hour. The conditions of work also varied enormously, with the larger non-profit homes providing career paths and encouragement through financial support for relevant qualifications.

Thus a division was starting to emerge between those 'core' homes providing adequate patterns of employment and those which fell beneath these standards. Here falling occupancy rates were leading to ever-worsening conditions of employment. In such cases staff appeared to be trapped in a downward cycle of poor pay, lack of support, shortage or absence of training and qualifications, and increased employment uncertainty.

Faced with these developments, it is interesting to consider the parallels between the changes in this market and those in the primary schools. If the introduction of privatization was intended to bolster the discipline of the market mechanisms within this sector, then it certainly reduced the number of operators in that market. If competition was reduced by this outcome then the government agencies were also confronted with a new responsibility for ensuring that quality standards and value for money were achieved.

The local authority had been transformed from a provider to a purchaser of services, as well as sustaining a monitoring role. As in the primary schools, the market as a competitive process composed of a multitude of equivalent players was a fiction. In the residential homes sector, the market had been maintained by extending the level of intervention through the creation of a complex and labour-intensive purchasing and monitoring role. With an increasing array of controls the ability of the smaller homes to survive was in doubt. As an article in the *Observer* newspaper suggested:

> new funding restraints will lead to receivership for 30% of Britain's 5,000 homes and challenges for some quoted companies.
>
> 'The process promises to be painful', says National Care Homes Association chief executive Sheila Scott. 'Homes of real quality could be forced to shut.'
>
> (Foster 1994)

With such pressures building within this sector the patterns of employment were likely to become greatly intensified, with some homes becoming 'sink' homes, some killed off by the market and the larger organizations able to exploit economies of scale to meet the statutory requirements. This recreation of a nineteenth-century market place in residential homes for the elderly unfortunately does not correspond to the idealized market notion of a multitude of independent operators.

Within the study group, the creation of a large monopoly resulting from the end of local authority homes had ensured that those within the sector were unable to compete, leaving many homes of 'real quality' in a position where their short-term survival appeared to be predicated upon their employees' need to tolerate evermore intensified forms of work. It is interesting to consider the extent to which this development may have been a sharper image of the process in train in teachers' work.

Drawing on the contributions of the theories of Fordism, post-Fordism, and neo-Fordism we have attempted to make a case for seeing similarities in patterns of restructuring. Though each theory can inform and illuminate particular facets of the restructuring of primary school teaching, the concepts, logic and vocabulary of the regulationists appear to offer a coherent account of the experiences captured by the research evidence.

Work and identity in the post-Fordist school

We have set out above the key reference points that have guided us in our attempt to make sense of changing primary schools using ideas current in the sociology of work and occupations. We have tried to show that we can trace a coherent pathway through regulation theory to marketization and thence to managerialism, and at key points in the text we have attempted to provide illuminative data from the education market-place in County Town. Some key areas merit further discussion, however.

Compliance, co-option, resistance: no escape from post-Fordist management?

In this section we want to consider the extent of managerial penetration of the working lives of teachers. There is always a danger that application of a labour process theory may call up images of (over)determining structures driving teachers towards proletarianized status. In reminding ourselves of the need to allow some autonomy and agency to these education workers, we should return to some of the arguments in Chapter 4, where the 'cycle' of teacher control was introduced. Hence it is not our intention to present our work as contributing to a revival of reproduction theory – though we do feel that the post-Fordist account ties education much more closely to the economy than hitherto. Nor is it our intention to present post-Fordist management as capitalism's final solution; indeed, we see it as very much part of a continuous flow of strategic developments designed to manage the inherent instability of professional work.

It is worth reiterating that strategies to ensure compliance from the teaching workforce have only limited success – hence the need to reformulate and redefine the strategies. It is also worth repeating that an important element in the instability in control of teaching is teachers' concept of education as entitlement, as public good, and their everyday actions in support of these positions. It is only within the theoretical terms set by the New Right that teachers may be seen as unproblematic technicians producing the new labour force. While we can identify the logic of this development in our analysis of market-driven trends in teachers' work, we neither defend it nor do we see its development as unproblematic. Indeed we hope to contribute to its problematization through our critique of the new managerialism and our depiction of its consequences.

It is worth remembering that the constant re-working of strategies for the control of teachers' work develops in response to the independent actions of teachers themselves, as well as in consequence of the contradictory functions of education systems. So teachers are not the mere recipients of policy, nor are they to be understood as endlessly manipulable. As we have indicated, they have strong work cultures and considerable loyalty and dedication to the education service. Again, as we have indicated in our earlier discussion of professionalism, this is at once a source of strength and a characteristic which renders them vulnerable to exploitation.

Drawing once again on Gramsci, we may wish to remind ourselves of the existence of the potential for counter-hegemony within any hegemonic discourse. George Riseborough has set out in diagrammatic form the repertoire of teacher responses to state policy (Figure 8.1).

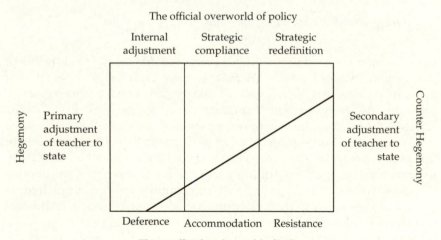

Figure 8.1   The repertoire of teacher negotiations and responses to state policy
Source: Riseborough (1993)

Identity and the restructuring of work

However, there remain elements of the new managerialism that may require serious consideration – and strategies of resistance if their impact is to be reduced. Some of these connect to the idea that new work processes are inevitable and also desirable (this is the 'positive' version of post-Fordism), so that defence of anything different looks like special pleading (the old charge against public sector bureaucracies) or a sort of Luddite defence of archaic and unproductive work processes. In this version of post-Fordist formations of teaching, the new professionalism on offer is one in which the teacher is integrated into the work system and there is no room to negotiate over fundamentals: 'autonomy is reduced and the commodity value of flexible specialism defines the very nature of the task' (Johnson 1989: 45).

We feel that the material we have presented here adds force to our (value-driven) concern with this research 'problem'. It may be helpful at this point to restate how we see the research 'puzzle'. We are concerned to understand the business of change in primary schooling in the context of marketization, and the consequent enhancement of managerialism and changes in primary teachers' work. Other research studies, based on much wider sampling than ours, suggest that explanations couched in terms of de-skilling and intensification look 'implausible' (Campbell and Neill 1994a), and set their explanations in terms of incomplete cultural change and teacher conscientiousness. Teachers, according to these studies, are identifying with reform to a degree. Some feel upskilled by the new processes, and any overwork and alienation may be attributed to the process of transition. In these explanations, the research problem is defined within the territorial boundaries of education, and without reference to wider debates; in Campbell and Neill's terms, there is 'a more cautious approach to theorising, based on more broadly-based observations of reality' (1994a: 214).

The material we have presented at intervals throughout the book, and our overall approach, suggest that a less cautious approach may have its uses. We suggest that apparent contradictions in primary teachers' reported experience of reform may be understood through appreciation of the co-optive force of the new managerial discourse, with its penetrative and persuasive power.

We have also argued for more attention to the gender dimension of this process of reform. The public and private accounts of the women teachers in our study are not, it could be argued, reflections of their confusion, or their conscientiousness (itself a very gendered term), or their false consciousness, nor yet entirely explicable through reference to incomplete processes of cultural change. Instead they may be understood as accurate reflections of the fragmented and fractured identities that are created by post-Fordist work forms, perhaps especially in the service professions, and perhaps especially for women workers.

We are indebted to Catherine Casey's (1995) work for our discussion here. She has very ably defended the significance of work – and research focused on work – as a central pillar in making sense of new formations of identity, and she supports her general argument through a case study of the 'Hephaestos' Corporation. She looked at the impact of the new managerialism on the workforce, with particular attention to the ways in which the new managerialism functions as a discursive social structure and process. She identifies different ways in which workers and managers accommodate to these new forms while attempting to protect their psychic health.

Casey makes some interesting observations about the adverse consequences of apparently benign upskilling work regimes. She points out that Fordist work forms offered the possibility of dissent, conflict and solidarity, and that those forms allowed workers to construct or preserve 'stronger measures of self and class defence' including alternative identities, for example, as public servants or experts within alienating bureaucratic regimes. She compares new work regimes to patriarchal families in their all-encompassing, but apparently benign and inclusive structures and processes. (This is a particularly interesting observation in view of the prevalence of male managers and female workforces in primary schools.)

Let us examine some of her conclusions about the general effects of these discourses of production:

1 Workers live in a state of *ambivalence* about the work and the new work culture. Ambivalence comes from the close *sociality* of teamwork, but the feeling that this is artificial and conceals competition and manoeuvring.
2 Workers are forced into accommodation and maturity through the *discipline* of teamwork, which harnesses their rational knowledge, technical skills and interpersonal skills, but denies and distorts *unnecessary* characteristics such as nurturance and patience.
3 The simulation of *relatedness*, and an over-emphasis on *competence*, combine to produce high levels of anxiety.

Once again we would draw attention to the consequences of importing a gender perspective on these effects.

These general effects produce particular responses from different self-types. Casey identifies defensive, colluded and capitulated selves. Defensive selves are angry, alienated and preoccupied with fighting further encroachment and with containing their anger. Colluded and capitulated selves form two sides of the same coin: the colluded self is the ideal form of the new worker, dependent, over-agreeable, compulsive in dedication and diligence, committed to the company. The obverse state of capitulation is characterized as follows:

> the self negotiates a private psychic settlement with the corporate colonising power . . . a wearied surrender . . . the possibilities of action are reduced as employee's previously semi-autonomous loci

of solidarity are taken over by the totalling corporate culture . . . the integrity of living one's life according to the calling of one's occupation is now denied . . .

(Casey 1995: 194–6)

We recognize those effects, and also recognize the defensive, capitulated and colluded selves that she identifies in response to managerialism. We would also acknowledge their presence in our own educational workplaces, and as part of our own identities.

9 CONCLUSION

In the previous chapter we returned to the informing theoretical framework from which we started on this task of making sense of primary schoolwork. Through the book there has been an attempt to create a dialogue between the detail of the fieldwork data and the overarching framework of the theoretically informed approach to the research.

We are cautious about 'summing up' our 'findings' because it is not in this mode that we have approached the task. Rather we have sought to illuminate a particular perspective on the changing work of primary teachers and managers, and to set that work in a larger theoretical and contextual framework. That approach has, we believe, permitted the construction of a coherent version of events. Some of the main elements of the narrative may be summarized as follows. In the first place, our assumption that there would be little evidence of a 'real' primary education market place is sustained by the enquiry into market activity in County Town. That led us into exploration of our related assumption about the significance of the market in changing relationships, and in destabilizing professional identities through a combination of internal and external pressures. From there we moved to a focus on the centrality of management in achieving this paradigm shift in professional identity, and to attention to the related experiences of stress, ambivalence and ambiguity in managerial and professional work in primary education.

The fieldwork, particularly the intensive case studies of Christchurch and Hill Edge schools, reveals institutional cultures undergoing major redefinition, at considerable personal cost to managers and workforce alike. It is apparent that the managers in our study felt levels of stress, ambiguity and ambivalence that paralleled the reported anxieties of the teachers. (See, for example, the material in Chapter 6 recording headteachers' difficulties in coping with the 'management' of their governing bodies.) We should also note the departure of experienced heads from the profession (Chapter 6, p. 93). Although there is some evidence of entrepreneurship of the kind identified by Halpin and Bell (1995), it is contradictory, in that the head that we selected as an exemplar of the new managerialism is far from content with his position; even someone who identifies with the direction of change is not comfortable with the personal cost and the disruption of the social relations of schoolwork. We make this point to underline our view that this interpretation of the redefinition of primary heads is not one in which they are cast as villains, seduced by HRM-speak into manipulating their staffs more effectively. There may be some who are riding the entrepreneurial wave without a backward glance (and we have a feeling that these will be men under 35), but the data we collected suggest a much more complex and conflicted response from those who are supposed to be benefiting from marketization. As in all areas of management under the new regimes of accumulation, there is a very considerable increase in responsibility concealed by the apparent flattening of hierarchies, and pressures for accountability produce greater isolation for the manager (Knights and Willmott 1989; Collinson and Collinson 1990).

We would also suggest that the evidence relating to teachers supports a reading of change in schoolwork connecting it to the broad strategies underlying post-Fordist work forms, particularly in their embodiment of anxiety and responsibility within the social relations of work itself. Primary schoolwork is no longer integrated, unalienated labour.

In this account of our work we have attempted a number of ambitious tasks. We wanted to investigate the operation of the market in primary schooling, paying particular attention to the impact of marketization on the internal processes of work in primary schools. We were interested to explore our assumptions about the limited nature of the education market in primary schooling, in order to establish whether the significance of the market lay more in the changes in work relations that it brought with it than in any enhancement of consumer choice. In particular we focused on the increased role and responsibility of management in delivering market-driven policy imperatives; we thought that it was possible to discern a paradigm shift in the nature of education management towards managerialism.

In carrying out our research, we accordingly identified a relatively discrete market in primary schooling, looked at the cultures and climates of a number of schools in response to marketization, and paid particular attention to the changing role of the primary head. We then focused down on two apparently contrasting schools, making an in-depth study of management/staff relations. This, then, is a straightforward account of our research project aims, and it would have been possible to present a similar account of our fieldwork that would have contributed to the emerging body of rich descriptions of life and work in the primary school. We have not chosen that route; rather we have attempted to juxtapose our fieldwork reporting with discussion of the framework of enquiry that has shaped our approach to the research. This is a relatively unusual procedure for reporting education research, where the convention is to introduce a theoretically-informed discussion of the data after the fact – that is after the fieldwork has been completed and reported. There is a dominant convention that the data are thus gathered 'objectively', rather than collected selectively to support some previously formed conception of how things may be.

We defended our departure from convention in the introductory chapter with reference to the following arguments. Firstly, it seems to us that it is reasonable to argue that there is a process of occupational restructuring going on from which education work is not excluded. Indeed we would go further, and support the analysis that identifies post-Fordist work formations as particularly significant in education, as education is itself a site of production of these forms. So our first claim is that it is reasonable and useful to look at what is going on in teaching from a perspective that is located beyond education and that places schoolwork in the frame with other forms of work and occupation. Secondly, we want to offer an alternative perspective on the research/theory relationship. It is apparent from our presentation of the data that we approached the study in a particular, theoretically-informed way. We have tried to make explicit the ways in which our understanding of marketization, and our view of the centrality of control of teachers' work, shaped our thinking about data collection and interpretation. We must emphazise that we do not claim to have 'proved' a post-Fordist 'hypothesis'; rather we hope to persuade our readers that this mode of research reporting is acceptable and illuminating, and that the combination of argument and data enable a particular reading of changes in primary schoolwork to be made. Thirdly, we wanted to engage in writing about research that moves away from the objective tradition in another way, through open identification with the people whose working lives we were investigating. We acknowledge our implication in the process that we have been studying, and our direct and complex engagement with it. We defend this stance on the grounds that the virtues of hygienic research are much exaggerated; indeed, we believe that our empathy with the people we were working with permitted us to see beyond the surface or 'public' accounts of their responses to change. We also acknowledge our own concerns about the damage being inflicted on education workers throughout the sector as a result of ideologically-driven change. We hope that our critical perspective on the new managerialism will reinforce strategies of resistance to it, and lend some support to education workers who feel themselves trapped in the ambivalence and ambiguity of post-Fordist work.

These, then, were our informing ideas in constructing the project, carrying out the research, and putting together this reported version of it. We hope that the detailed accounts of schoolwork, together with the discussion of the main contributing ideas in the framework that shaped the research, produce a 'good, persuasive and by and large reasonable case' (Casey 1995: 198).

REFERENCES

Acker, S. (1990) Teachers' culture in an English primary school: continuity and change, *British Journal of Sociology of Education*, 11(3), 257–73.

Adler, M. (1993) An alternative approach to parental choice, in *Briefings for the Paul Hamlyn Foundation National Commission on Education*. London: Heinemann.

Adler, M., Petch, A. and Tweedie, J. (1989) *Parental Choice and Educational Policy*. Edinburgh: Edinburgh University Press.

Adler, M. and Raab, C. (1988) Exit, choice and loyalty: the impact of parental choice on admission to primary schools, *Journal of Education Policy*, 3(2): 115–81.

Aglietta, N. (1976) *The Theory of Capitalist Regulation*. London: New Left Books.

Apple, M. (1988) Work, class and teaching, in J. Ozga (ed.) *Schoolwork*. Milton Keynes: Open University Press.

Arnold, M. (1862) The twice-revised code, *Frazer's Magazine*. London.

Atkinson, J. (1984) Manpower strategies for flexible organisation, *Personnel Management* August: 27–31.

Bagguley, P. (1991) Post-Fordism and enterprise culture, in R. Keat and N. Abercrombie (eds) *Enterprise Culture*. London: Routledge.

Ball, S. (1990) *Politics and Policy Making in Education*. London: Routledge.

Ball, S. (1993a) Changing management and the management of change: education reform and the schooling process, an English perspective. Paper to AERA Annual Conference, San Francisco.

Ball, S. (1993b) Education, Majorism and the curriculum of the dead, *Curriculum Studies*, 1(2): 195–215.

Ball, S. (1994) *Education Reform: A Critical and Post-Structural Approach*. Buckingham: Open University Press.

Barker, A. (ed.) (1982) *Quangos in Britain: Government and the Networks of Public Policy-Making*. London: Macmillan.

Bartlett, W., Propper, C., Wilson, D. and Le Grand, J. (eds) (1994) *Quasi-Markets in the Welfare State*. Bristol: School of Advanced Urban Studies.

Black, E. (1996) Managing to change? The role of the primary school head, in P. Croll (ed.) *Teachers, Pupils and Primary Schooling: Continuity and Change*. London: Cassell.

Blyton, P. and Turnbull, P. (1992) *Reassessing Human Resource Management*. London: Sage.

Bottery, M. (1995) Professionalism, a comparative study. Paper to European Conference on Educational Research, University of Bath, 14–17 September.

Bourdieu, P., Chambored, J. and Passeron, J.L. (1991) *The Craft of Sociology: Epistemological Preliminaries*. Paris: Dr. Gruyter.

Bowe, R. and Ball, S., with Gold, A. (1992) *Reforming Education and Changing Schools: Case Studies in Policy Sociology*. London: Routledge.

Bowe, R., Ball, S. and Gewirtz, S. (1994) Captured by the discourse? Issues and concerns in researching 'parental choice', *British Journal of Sociology of Education*, 15(1): 63–78.

Bowles, S. and Gintis, H. (1976) *Schooling in Capitalist America*. London: Routledge & Kegan Paul.

Boyer, R. (1990) *The Regulation School: A Critical Introduction*. New York: Columbia University Press.

Braverman, H. (1974) *Labour and Monopoly Capital. The Degradation of Work in the Twentieth Century*. New York: Monthly Review Press.

Broadfoot, P. and Pollard, A. (1996) Continuity and change in English primary education, in P. Croll (ed.) *Teachers, Pupils and Primary Schooling: Continuity and Change*. London: Cassell.

Brown, P. and Lauder, H. (1992) *Education for Economic Survival: from Fordism to post-fordism?* London: Routledge.

Burgess, H., Southworth, G. and Webb, R. (1994) Whole school planning in the primary school, in A. Pollard (ed.) *Look Before You Leap – Research Evidence for the Curriculum at Key Stage 2*. London: Tufnell Press.

Caldwell, B. and Spinks, J. (1992) *Leading the Self Managing School*. Lewes: Falmer Press.

Campbell, J. and Neill, S.R (1994a) *Curriculum Reform at Key Stage One*, Harlow: Longman.

Campbell, J. and Neill, S.R. (1994b) *Primary Teachers at Work*. London: Routledge.

Casey, C. (1995) *Work, Self and Society after Industrialism*. London: Routledge.

Collinson, D. and Collinson, M. (1990) *Managing to Discriminate*. London: Routledge.

Commission on Excellence in Education (1988) *A Nation at Risk*.

Connell, R. (1985) *Teachers' Work*. London: George Allen & Unwin.

Connell, R. (1995) *Masculinities*. Cambridge: Polity Press.

Cox, R. (1980) Social forces, states and world orders, *Millennium: Journal of International Studies*, 10(2): 126–55.

Cox, B. and Dyson, A. (1969) *The Black Papers*. London: Critical Quarterly.

Dale, R. (1981) Control, accountability and William Tyndale, in R. Dale *et al.* (eds) *Education and the State*, vol. 2: *Politics, Patriarchy and Practice*. Lewes: Falmer Press.

Dale, R. (1994) Marketing the education market and the polarisation of schooling, in D. Kallos and S. Lindblad (eds) *New Policy Contexts for Education: Sweden and the United Kingdom*. Umea: Umea Universitat.

Dale, R. (1989a) *The State and Education Policy*. Buckingham: Open University Press.

Dale, R. (1989b) The Thatcherite project in education, *Critical Social Policy*, 9(3): 26–33.

Deem, R., Brehoney, K. and Heath, S. (1995) *Active Citizenship and the Governing of Schools*. Buckingham: Open University Press.

Dunleavy, P. and O'Leary, B. (1987) *Theories of the State: The politics of Liberal Democracy*. London: Macmillan.

Ferner, A. (1995) The role of the state, in R. Hyman and A. Ferner (eds) *New Frontiers in European Industrial Relations*. Oxford: Blackwell.

Flynn, R. (1993) *Structures of Control in Health Management*. London: Routledge.

Foster, M. (1994) Nursing home owners lick their wounds, *The Observer*, 30 January.

Frances, J. (1994) Introduction, in G. Thompson, J. Frances, R. Levačić and J. Mitchell (eds) *Markets, Hierarchies and Networks: The Coordination of Social Life*. London: Sage.

Freedman, S. (1988) Teacher 'burnout' and institutional stress, in J. Ozga (ed.) *Schoolwork*. Milton Keynes: Open University Press

Fulcher, J. (1991) *Labour Movements, Employers and the State: Conflict and Co-operation*. Oxford: Oxford University Press.

Fullan, M. and Hargreaves, A. (1992) *What's Worth Fighting For in Your School?* Buckingham: Open University Press.

Gamble, A. (1994) *Willing Slaves: British Workers under HRM*. Cambridge: University Press.

Geary, J. (1992) Employment, flexibility and HRM, *Work, Employment and Society*, 6(2): 251–70.

Gewirtz, S. (1994) Market disciplines versus comprehensive education, in D. Kallos and S. Lindblad (eds) *New Policy Contexts for Education: Sweden and the United Kingdom*. Umea: Umea Universitat.

Gewirtz, S. (1995) Choice, equity and control in education. Paper to Second Comparative Education Policy Seminar: Sweden and England, London, April.

Gewirtz, S., Ball, S.J. and Bowe, R. (1995) *Markets, Choice and Equity in Education*. Buckingham: Open University Press.

Gewirtz, S. and Ozga, J. (1990) Partnership, pluralism and education policy: a reassessment, *Journal of Education Policy*, 5(1): 37–48.

Glennerster, H. (1991) Quasi-markets and education, *Economic Journal*, 101: 16–25.

Goodwin, E., and Le Grand, J. (1987) *Not Only the Poor: The Middle Class and Welfare*. London: Allen & Unwin.

Grace, G. (1985) Judging teachers: the social and political contexts of teacher evaluation, *British Journal of the Sociology of Education*, Vol. 6(1).

Grace, G. (1987) Teachers and the state, in M. Lawn and G. Grace (eds) *Teachers: The Culture and Politics of Work*. London: Falmer Press.

Grace, G. (1995) *Beyond Educational Leadership*. Lewes: Falmer Press.

Gramsci, A. (1971) *Selection from the Prison Notebooks*. London: Lawrence and Wishart.

Graystone, J. (1995) Beyond our ken, *Times Educational Supplement*, 9 June, p. 8.

Grumet, M. (1994) Conception, contradiction and curriculum, in L. Stone (ed.) *The Education Feminism Reader*. London: Routledge.

Hall, S. (1988) Brave New World, *Marxism Today*, October.

Halpin, D. and Bell, L. (1995) Managing self-governing primary schools in the locally managed, grant-maintained and private sectors: contrasts and continuities. Paper to Managing Autonomous Schools Symposium, European Conference on Educational Research, University of Bath, 14–17 September.

Hargreaves, A. (1994) *Changing Teachers, Changing Times: Teachers' Work and Culture in the Post-Modern Age*. London: Cassell.

Hargreaves, D. and Hopkins, D. (1991) *The Empowered School*. London: Cassell.

Hartley, D (1994) Devolved school management: the 'new deal' in Scottish education, *Journal of Education Policy*, 9(2): 129–41.

Harvey, D. (1990) *The Condition of Postmodernity*. Oxford: Blackwell.

Hatcher, R. (1994) Market relationships and the management of teachers, *British Journal of Sociology of Education*, 15(1), 41–61.

Hellawell, D. (1991) The changing role of the head in the primary school in England, *School Organisation*, 11(3), 321–37.

Hickox, M. and Moore, R. (1992) Education and post-Fordism: a new correspondence, in P. Brown and H. Launder (eds) *Education for Economic Survival*. London: Routledge.

Hood, C. (1991) *The New Public Sector Management*. London: Routledge.

Hoyle, E. and John, P. (1995) *Professional Knowledge and Professional Practice*. London: Cassell.

Hyman, R. (1991) The theory of production and the production of theory, in A. Pollert (ed.) *Farewell to Flexibility*. Oxford: Blackwell.

Jessop, B. (1988) Regulation theory, post-Fordism and the state: more than a reply to Werner Bonefield, *Capital and Class*, 34: 147–68.

Jessop, B. (1990) Regulation theories in retrospect and prospect, *Economy and Society*, 9(2): 153–216.

Jessop, S. (1990) *State Theory*. New York: Penn State University.

Johnson (1989) Thatcherism and English education: breaking the mould or confirming the pattern?, *History of Education*, 18(2): 91–121.

Jonathon, R. (1990) State education service or prisoner's dilemma? *Educational Philosophy and Theory*, 22(1): 16–24.

Jones, G. and Hayes, D. (1991) Primary headteachers and ERA two years on: the pace of change and its impact upon schools, *School Organisation*, 11(2): 211–21.

Keep, E. (1992) Schools in the marketplace? Some problems with private sector models, *British Journal of Education and Work*, 5(2): 43–56.

Kenway, J. (ed.) (1994) *Economising Education: Post-Fordist Directions*. Deakin: Deakin University Press.

Kickert, W. (1991) Steering at a distance: a new paradigm for public governance in Dutch higher education. Paper to European Consortium for Educational Research, University of Essex.

Knights, D. and Willmott, H. (1989) Power and subjectivity at work: from degradation to subjugation in social relations, *Sociology*, 23(4): 45–63.

Landman, M. and Ozga, J. (1995) Teacher education policy in England, in M. Ginsburg and B. Linsday (eds) *The Political Dimension in Teacher Education*. London: Falmer Press.

Larson, M. (1977) *The Rise of the Professions: A Sociological Analysis*. Berkeley: University of California Press.

Law, J. (1994) *Organising Modernity*. Cambridge: Polity Press.

Lawn, M. (1987) *Servants of the State: The Contested Control of Teaching, 1910–1930*. Lewes: Falmer Press.

Lawn, M. and Mac an Ghaill, M. (1994) Primary schoolwork, Paper to CEDAR Conference, Warwick University.

Lawn, M. and Ozga, J. (1981) *Teachers, Professionalism and Class*. Lewes: Falmer Press.

Lawn, M. and Ozga, J. (1986) Unequal partners: teachers under indirect rule, *British Journal of the Sociology of Education*, 7(2): 225–38.

Le Bier, D. (1986) *Modern Madness: The Hidden Link Between Work and Emotional Conflict*. New York: Simon and Schuster.

Le Grand, J. (1991) Quasi-markets and social policy, *Economic Journal*, 101: 1256–67.

Le Grand, J. and Bartlett, W. (eds) (1993) *Quasi-Markets and Social Policy*. London: Macmillan.

Legge, K. (1993) Human resource management: a critical analysis, in J. Storey (ed.) *New Perspectives on Human Resource Management*. London: Routledge.

Levačić, R. (1994) Markets and government: an overview, in G. Thompson, J. Frances, R. Levačić and J. Mitchell (eds) *Markets, Hierarchies and Networks: The Coordination of Social Life*. London: Sage.

Littler, C. (1982) *The Development of the Labour Process in Capitalist Societies*. London: Heinemann.

McCallum, B., McAlister, S., Brown, M. and Gipps, C. (1993) Teacher assessment at key stage?, *Research Papers in Education Policy and Practice*, 8(3): 305–28.

MacDonald, K. (1995) *The Sociology of the Professions*. London: Sage.

MacGilchrist, B., Mortimore, P., Savage, J. and Beresford, C. (1995) *Planning Matters: The Impact of Development Planning in Primary Schools*. London: Paul Chapman Press.

Miller, S. and Rose, N. (1994) On therapeutic authority: psychoanalytical expertise under advanced liberalism, *History of Human Sciences*, 7(3): 29–64.

Mortimore, J. and Mortimore, P. (1991) *The Primary Head – Roles, Responsibilities and Reflections*. London: Paul Chapman.

Newman, E. and Pollard, A. (1994) From conflict to co-operation? Observing change in primary schools, in D. Hargreaves and D. Hopkins (eds) *Issues in School Development Planning*. London: Falmer.

Nias, J. (1989) *Primary Teachers Talking*. London: Routledge.

Nias, J., Southworth, G. and Yeomans, R. (1989) *Staff Relationships in the Primary School*. London: Cassell.

O'Connor, D. (1973) *The Fiscal Crisis of The State*. New York: St Martins Press.

Osborn, M. (1996) Changes in teachers' professional perspectives at Key Stage 1, in P. Croll (ed.) *Teachers, Pupils and Primary Schooling: Continuity and Change*. London: Cassell.

Ozga, J.T. (1988) Teachers' work and careers, Unit W1 of Open University Course EP228 *Frameworks for Teaching*. Milton Keynes: Open University.

Ozga, J.T. (1990) A social danger: the contested history of teacher–state relations, in L. Jamieson and H. Corr (eds) *State, Private Life and Political Change*. London: Macmillan.

Ozga, J.T. and Lawn, M. (1981) *Teachers, Professionalism and Class*. Lewes: Falmer Press.

Ozga, J. and Lawn, M. (1988) Schoolwork: interpreting the labour process of teaching, *British Journal of the Sociology of Education*, 9(3): 323–36.

Piore, M. and Sabel, C. (1984) *The Second Industrial Divide: Possibilities for Prosperity*. New York: Basic Books.

Pitner, N. (1981) Hormones and harems: are the activities of superintending different for women? in P. Schmuck *et al.* (eds) *Education Policy and Management: Sex Differentials*. New York: Academic Press.

Pollard, A. (1985) *The Social World of the Primary School*. London: Cassell.

Pollard, A., Croll, P., Broadfoot, P., Osborne, M. and Abbott, D. (1994) *Changing English Primary Schools?* London: Cassell.

Pollert, A. (ed.) (1991) *Farewell to Flexibility?* Oxford: Blackwell.

Proctor, N. (ed.) (1990) *The Aims of Primary Education and the National Curriculum*. Lewes: Falmer Press.

Raab, C. (1991) Education policy and management: contemporary changes in Britain, Paper to International Institute of Administrative Sciences, Copenhagen, July.

Riseborough, G. (1993) Primary headship, state policy and the challenge of the 1990s: an exceptional story that disproves total hegemonic rule, *Journal of Education Policy*, 8(2): 155–73.

Roberts, H. (1993) *Doing Feminist Research*. London: Routledge.

Saran, R. and Busher, H. (1995) Working with support staff in schools, in H. Busher and R. Saran (eds) *Managing Teachers as Professionals in Schools*. London: Kogan Page.

School Teachers Review Body (1993) *Second Annual Report*. London: HMSO.

School Teachers Review Body (1994) *Third Annual Report*. London: HMSO.

Scott, A. (1994) *Willing Slaves? British Workers under Human Resource Management*. Cambridge: Cambridge University Press.

Seddon, T. (1996) The principle of choice in policy research, in *Journal of Education Policy*, 11(2): 197–125.

Seifert, R. (1987) *Teacher Militancy*. Lewes: Falmer Press.

Shakeshaft, C. (1989) *Women in Educational Administration*. London: Sage.

Sharp, R. and Green A. with Lewis, J. (1975) *Education and Social Control*. London: Routledge & Kegan Paul.

Shilling, C. (1989) The mini-enterprise in schools project, a new stage in education–industry relations? *Journal of Education Policy*, 4(2): 115–25.

Sisson, K. (1995) Paradigms, practice and prospects, in K. Sisson (ed.) *Personnel Management – A Comprehensive Guide to Theory and Practice in Britain*. Oxford: Blackwell.

Smith, A. (1973) *The Concept of Social Change: A Critique of the Functionalist Theory of Social Change*. London: Routledge & Kegan Paul.

Soucek, V. (1994) Flexible education and new standards of communicating competence, in J. Kenway (ed.) *Economising Education: Post-Fordist Directions*. Geelong, Australia: Deakin University Press.

Stanley, L. and Wise, S. (1993) *Breaking Out Again*, 2nd edn. London: Routledge.

Storey, J. (ed.) (1989) *New Perspectives on Human Resource Management*. London: Routledge.

Taylor, F. (1947) *Scientific Management*. New York: Harper and Row.

Thomas, H. (1994) Markets, collectivities and management, *Oxford Review of Education*, 20(1):84–93.

Thompson, P. and McHugh, D. (1995) *Work Organisation, A Critical Introduction* (2nd Edn). London: Macmillan.

Troyna, B. (1994) Critical social research and education policy, *British Journal of Education Studies*, 42(1): 52–71.

Walkerdine, V. (1983) It's only natural: rethinking child-centred pedagogy, in A. Wolpe and J. Donald (eds.) *Is There Anyone Here From Education?* London: Pluto Press.

Wallace, M. (1992) Coping with multiple innovations: an exploratory study, *School Organisation*, 11(2), 187–209.

Watkins, P. (1994) The Fordist/Post-Fordist Debate: the educational implications, in J. Kenway (ed.) *Economising Education: Post-Fordist Directions*. Geelong, Australia: Deakin University Press.

Webb, R. and Vulliamy, G. (1996) *Roles and Responsibilities in the Primary School*. Buckingham: Open University Press.

Weinstock, A. (1976) I blame the teachers, *Times Educational Supplement*, 24 January.

Whitty, G. (1989) The new right and the national curriculum: state control or market forces?, in M. Flude and M. Hammer (eds) *The Education Reform Act 1988*. London: Falmer Press.

Whitty, G. and Menter, I. (1991) The progress of restructuring, in D. Coulby and L. Bash, *Contradiction and Conflict in the 1988 Education Act*. London: Cassell.

Williams, K., Haslam, J., Williams, T. and Cutler, T. (1992) Ford-v-'Fordism': the beginning of mass production, *Work, Employment and Society*, 6(1): 517–48.

Woods, P. (1995) *Creative Teachers in the Primary School*. Buckingham: Open University Press.

Yeatman, C. (1990) *Bureaucrats, Technocrats, Femocrats: Essays on the Contemporary Australian State*. Sydney: Allen & Unwin.

Index

MARKETS, CHOICE AND EQUITY IN EDUCATION

Sharon Gewirtz, Stephen J. Ball and Richard Bowe

- What has been the impact of parental choice and competition upon schools?
- How do parents choose schools for their children?
- Who are the winners and losers in the education market?

These important and fundamental questions are discussed in this book which draws upon a three year intensive study of market forces in education. The authors carefully examine the complexities of parental choice and school responses to the introduction of market forces in education. Particular attention is paid to issues of opportunity and equity, and patterns of access and involvement related to gender, ethnicity and social class are identified.

This is the first comprehensive study of market dynamics in education and it highlights the specificity and idiosyncrasies of local education markets. However, the book is not confined to descriptions of these markets but also offers a systematic theorization of the education market, its operation and consequences. It will be of particular interest to students on BEd and Masters courses in education, headteachers and senior managers in schools, and policy analysts.

Contents
Researching education markets – Choice and class: parents in the marketplace – An analysis of local market relations – Managers and markets: school organization in transition – Schooling in the marketplace: a semiological analysis – Internal practices: institutional responses to competition – Choice, equity and control – Glossary of terms – References – Index.

224pp   0 335 19369 2 (Paperback)   0 335 19370 6 (Hardback)